Contents

Frontispiece: a detail from "Father Hennepin and His Two Men Made Prisoners by the Sioux, on the Mississippi, April, 1680", painted by George Catlin in 1847.

Left: an Indian from the Nipissing region, Canada, drawn by an anonymous artist in Canada, in 1717.

List of Maps

The illuminated globe shows in blue
the areas of North America opened up
by Spanish, French, and English
explorers between the arrival of
Columbus in 1492 and the Louisiana
Purchase in 1803—the period covered
by this book.

RIVERS OF DESTINY

DISCOVERY AND EXPLORATION

International Learning Systems Corporation Limited · London

RIVERS OF DESTINY

BY SIMON DRESNER

Executive Coordinators: Beppie Harrison
                        John Mason
Design Director: Guenther Radtke
Editorial: Ann Craig
           Damian Grint
           Marjorie Dickens
Picture Editor: Peter Cook
Research: Enid Moore
          Sarah Waters
Cartography by Geographical Projects

This edition specially produced in 1973
for International Learning Systems
Corporation Limited, London
by Aldus Books Limited, London.

Printed and bound in Yugoslavia by
Mladinska Knjiga, Ljubljana

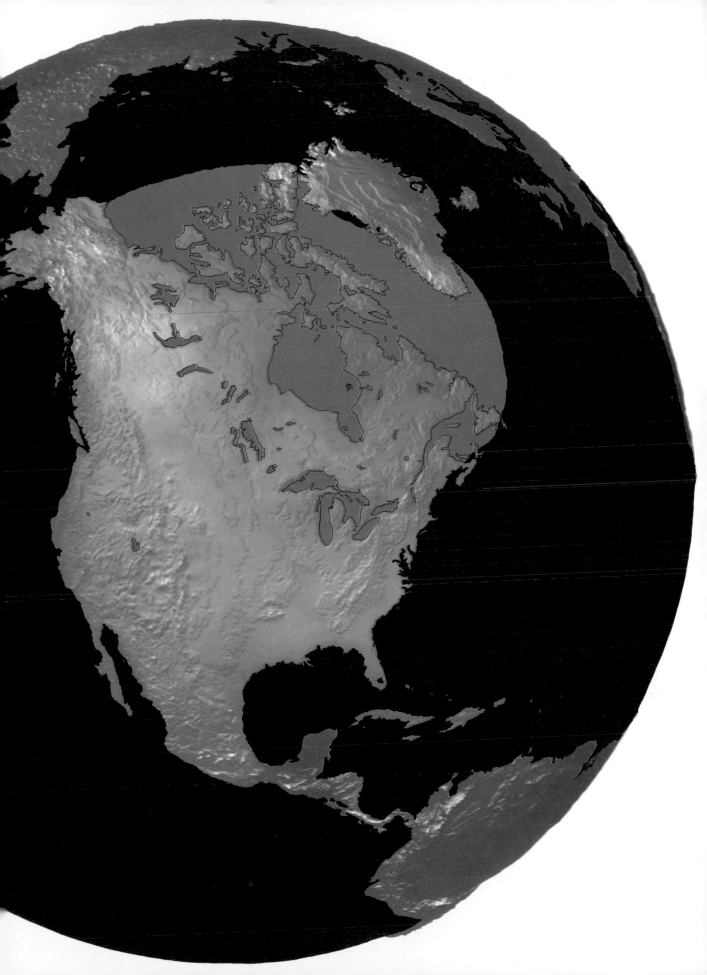

The First Americans
1

In the early hours of October 12, 1492, three small, weather-beaten ships moved slowly westward through the waters of the Atlantic. The night was calm, but the men on board the three vessels tossed restlessly in their sleep. They had been sailing through uncharted seas for more than a month, and most of the crew shared a deep and fearful conviction that they were doomed. Their commander's promises that they would find "lands to the west" had begun to sound like the words of a madman, and mutiny was brewing. . . .

Suddenly, at 2 A.M., a hoarse shout rang out from the watch on board the *Pinta*. "Land!" cried the lookout, "Land! Land!" The ship's master, Captain Martin Pinzon, hurriedly made his way to the rails and peered through the mist. It was not the first time that "land" had been sighted in the last two weeks, and he feared what the crew might do if their frail hopes were dashed again. But this time there could be no mistake. Land lay ahead, a pale but distinct line low on the horizon. He could just make out a row of white cliffs shining far away in the moonlight.

News of the sighting quickly passed from ship to ship. As the excited crews made preparations for a landing, Admiral Christopher

Left: the people of the vast new world that Columbus discovered were not mere savages, who had no experience of any culture but their own, as reported by the early explorers. American "Indians" were in fact an enormously varying people, with patterns of life adapted harmoniously to the conditions in which they lived. In this painting George Catlin shows the Chippewa dancing their snowshoe dance, singing in thanksgiving to the Great Spirit for the first snowfall, when hunters could track their quarry more easily.

Right: Christopher Columbus, in a portrait by Sebastiano de Piombo, painted in 1519, probably from a life portrait. It shows Columbus in his vigorous and commanding middle age.

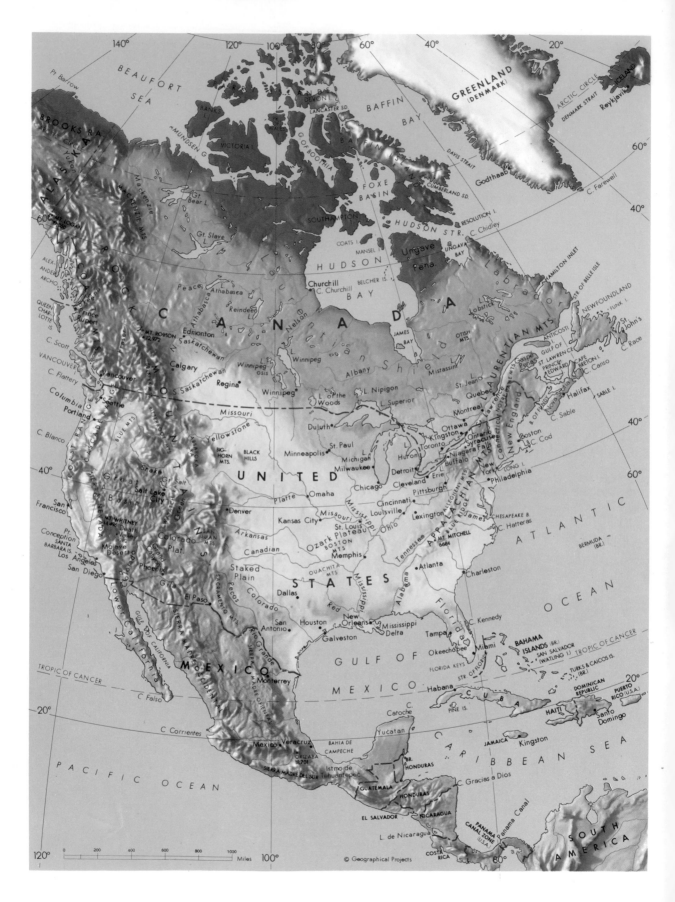

PACIFIC OCEAN

ATLANTIC OCEAN

BEAUFORT SEA

GREENLAND (DENMARK)

ICELAND

Reykjavik

ARCTIC CIRCLE

DENMARK STRAIT

BAFFIN BAY

DAVIS STRAIT

C. Farewell

Godthaab

Pt. Barrow

BROOKS RA.

ALASKA

MT. OGDEN

BANKS I.

VICTORIA I.

AMUNDSEN G.

GULF OF BOOTHIA

DEVON I.

LANCASTER SD.

PR. OF WALES I.

BAFFIN ISLAND

CUMBERLAND SD.

RESOLUTION I.

HUDSON STR.

C. Chidley

FOXE BASIN

SOUTHAMPTON I.

COATS I.

MANSEL I.

BELCHER IS.

Ungava Pen.

UNGAVA BAY

HAMILTON INLET

STR. OF BELLE ISLE

MACKENZIE MTS.

Gt. Bear L.

Gt. Slave L.

HUDSON BAY

JAMES BAY

Labrador

NEWFOUNDLAND

FUNK I.

C A N A D A

Peace

Athabasca

L. Athabasca

Reindeer

Churchill

C. Churchill

Nelson

OTISH MTS.

St. John's

C. Race

ALEX. ARCH.

ANDER. ARCH.

QUEEN CHARLOTTE IS.

Skeena

Prince Rupert

C. Scott

MT. ROBSON 12,972

Edmonton

Saskatchewan

L. Winnipegosis

Albany

L. Mistassini

Laurentian Shield

ANTICOSTI

GULF OF ST. LAWRENCE

PRINCE EDWARD I.

CAPE BRETON I.

C. Canso

VANCOUVER I.

C. Flattery

Vancouver

Seattle

Columbia

Portland

C. Blanco

Calgary

S. Saskatchewan

Regina

Winnipeg

L. Winnipeg

Missouri

L. of the Woods

L. Nipigon

Duluth

L. Superior

Quebec

Montreal

Ottawa

St. Jean

St. Lawrence

New England

Halifax

NOVA SCOTIA

C. Sable

SABLE I.

Yellowstone

St. Paul

Minneapolis

L. Huron

L. Michigan

Toronto

L. Ontario

Kingston

Syracuse

Niagara Falls

Buffalo

New York

LONG I.

Boston

C. Cod

BLUE MTS.

BIG HORN MTS.

BLACK HILLS

Milwaukee

Chicago

Detroit

L. Erie

Cleveland

Pittsburgh

Philadelphia

CONNECTICUT

ALLEGHENY MTS.

U N I T E D

Great Basin

Salt Lake City

Gt. Salt L.

Platte

Omaha

Cincinnati

Louisville

Lexington

James

CHESAPEAKE B.

San Francisco

MT. WHITNEY 14,495

Death Valley

Denver

Missouri

Kansas City

St. Louis

Ohio

APPALACHIAN

BLUE RIDGE

C. Hatteras

BERMUDA (BR.)

Pt. Conception

SANTA BARBARA IS.

Los Angeles

San Diego

Mojave Desert

SAN JUAN MTS.

Colorado Plat.

Arkansas

Canadian

Ozark Plateau

BOSTON MTS.

Memphis

Tennessee

MT. MITCHELL 6684

Atlanta

Charleston

SIERRA NEVADA

Snake

Gila

Phoenix

Staked Plain

OUACHITA MTS.

S T A T E S

ATLANTIC OCEAN

San Antonio

Dallas

Pecos

Colorado

Red

Mississippi

Alabama

Florida

El Paso

Rio Grande

Houston

Galveston

New Orleans

Mississippi Delta

Tampa

C. Kennedy

SACRAMENTO MTS.

SIERRA MADRE OCCIDENTAL

M E X I C O

GULF OF CALIFORNIA

Lower California

Okeechobee

L. Okeechobee

Miami

FLORIDA KEYS

BAHAMA ISLANDS (BR.)

SAN SALVADOR (WATLING I.)

TROPIC OF CANCER

TURKS & CAICOS IS. (BR.)

TROPIC OF CANCER

C. Falso

Monterrey

SIERRA MADRE ORIENTAL

M E X I C O

Habana

STR. OF FLORIDA

C U B A

PINE IS.

HAITI

DOMINICAN REPUBLIC

PUERTO RICO (U.S.A.)

Santo Domingo

C. Corrientes

Mexico

Veracruz

ORIZABA 18,701

BAHIA DE CAMPECHE

Yucatan

C. Catoche

JAMAICA

Kingston

CARIBBEAN SEA

SIERRA MADRE DEL SUR

Istmo de Tehuantepec

BR. HONDURAS

C. Gracias a Dios

GUATEMALA

HONDURAS

EL SALVADOR

NICARAGUA

L. de Nicaragua

PANAMA CANAL ZONE U.S.A.

Panama Canal

COSTA RICA

SOUTH AMERICA

PACIFIC OCEAN

0   200   400   600   800   1000
Miles

© Geographical Projects

140°   120°   100°   80°   60°   40°   20°

60°   40°   60°   40°   20°

120°   100°   60°

Columbus paced the deck of the Spanish flagship *Santa María* in eager anticipation. Not for a moment did either he or his men doubt that the island now looming up before them was an outpost of the fabled Indies, the Eastern world of spice and treasure, luxury and culture so glowingly described by Marco Polo.

That the world he had discovered was utterly different from what he believed it to be would not in fact be fully realized for almost a decade. Columbus himself would never know that he had found the New World and that, in so doing, he had inaugurated a period of exploration, conquest, and colonization that would completely alter the course of history.

But if Columbus was ignorant of the real significance of his voyage, so too were the peoples who would ultimately be most affected by it. As the three ships moved slowly, fatefully, toward the island of San Salvador in the Bahamas, neither its inhabitants nor those of the immense continent beyond it had any inkling of the dramatic

Above: Osceola, the young warrior of the Seminole tribe, shows all the pride and distinguished bearing of the native Americans in this portrait painted by George Catlin in 1837–38.

Right: the Indian village of Secoton, Virginia, showing the tidy arrangement of fields and houses. The watercolor drawing is by John White, the leader of the ill-fated colony of Roanoke.

changes that lay in store for them. On that continent in the early hours of October 12, 1492, the descendants of the New World's first discoverers and settlers slept quietly. They would not know about Columbus for decades, in some cases for centuries. And had they known, they could not have guessed that the three tiny ships now making for a Caribbean island were the harbingers of a new era —an era in which they and their way of life would be threatened, and in many tragic cases destroyed.

Who were these million or so people who occupied the North American continent at the time of Columbus' arrival? In his mistaken belief that he had reached the Indies, Columbus called the islanders "Indians," and the term was later applied to the native inhabitants of North and South America as well. In fact, the American Indians *are* related to the people of Asia but only distantly, and far back in the mists of time.

The original ancestors of the American Indians came from northeast Asia. They were primitive hunting peoples who, more than 20,000 years ago, began crossing from Siberia into Alaska over a broad land bridge now covered by the waters of the Bering Strait. Successive waves of these nomadic peoples gradually moved farther south and east in search of better hunting grounds. Over thousands of years, their descendants ultimately spread out across North America and down through Central and South America. Gradually, each group's adaptation to the climate, geography, and food resources of its own particular region affected not only the type of tools, clothing, and shelter it developed, but also its social organization, customs, beliefs—even its appearance. So, by the time Columbus arrived, the two continents contained not one, but many separate peoples. In North America alone, there were at least 600 different tribes, speaking over 200 distinct languages, and following ways of life as richly diverse as the regions they occupied.

A great many of these North American tribes inhabited the extensive forests that covered almost the entire eastern half of the continent. Collectively, they are known today as the Eastern Forests Indians, but because they followed a number of distinctly different life styles, they are often divided into three major groups.

The most northerly of these groups, the Subarctic Hunters, were nomadic tribes like the Beaver, Carrier, Kutchin, and Cree of west and eastern Canada. Following the seasonal migrations of caribou and moose, they were constantly on the move, traveling in large, light birchbark canoes, or on foot—using snowshoes or toboggans in wintertime. The subarctic Indians were a proud and independent people who inhabited a harsh and inhospitable world. The terribly cold winters and ever-present threat of death by starvation made some of them ruthlessly practical. It was common among some of the northern tribes, for example, to abandon the old and the sick when they could no longer keep up with their families.

A very different group of Eastern Forests Indians lived south of the Canadian border. These, the Northeastern Woodsmen, are

Above: the Indian method of hunting deer, as reported by Jacques le Moyne de Morgues, one of the members of the French expedition to Florida in 1564. He explained that the hunter's head fitted into the head of the animal, peering out of the holes where the deer's eyes had been "as through a mask."

Left: the ingenuity of the American Indians in finding practical methods of catching food, lacking the metals so common in Europe, fascinated the early visitors to America. Here John White carefully recorded how the Indians he saw in Virginia in 1585 caught fish.

among the best known of America's Indians, for they played a crucial role in its early exploration and colonization. It was to this group of tribes, too, that one of the most interesting prehistoric Indian peoples belonged. These were the Hopewell Indians, who flourished in the Ohio Valley region from about 1000 B.C. to about A.D. 1300, and formed part of the so-called Mound Builder culture. Farmers, traders, and skilled craftsmen, the Hopewells operated an extraordinary network of trade that brought them into contact with other tribes from coast to coast. It was the Hopewells who built the many dome-shaped burial mounds and curious animal-shaped mounds that can still be seen in the Ohio Valley states today.

Above: fortitude in suffering was one of the most highly prized virtues for many Indian tribes. The Mandan had a grueling religious torture ceremony, shown here, in which their young men took part to prove their courage. When George Catlin, who painted this scene, reported the ceremonies his account was so horrifying that for years many people simply refused to believe him.

Right: a wampum belt and two bracelets. For the Iroquois, as for some of their neighboring tribes, these were not for decoration, but were used as money.

But in 1492, the region once dominated by the Hopewell people had long since been occupied by other tribes, such as the Shawnee. Around the Great Lakes, dwelt the Menominee, Fox, Illinois, Sauk, Winnebago, and Potawatomi. Most of these Great Lakes Indians spoke variations of the Algonkian tongue, a language also spoken by the tribes who lived along the Atlantic coastline from present-day Maine to the Carolinas. These tribes—the Micmac, Penobscot, Massachusett, Pequot, Delaware, and Powhatan—were the very first Indians met by the early explorers.

Between the Algonkian-speaking Indians of the Great Lakes and those of the Atlantic seaboard lived five tribes who spoke another language altogether. These were the famous Iroquois—the Cayuga, Oneida, Seneca, Mohawk, and Onondaga—who made their homes in upstate New York. In addition to their distinctive language, the Iroquois had developed a unique type of dwelling. Unlike the round or oval bark-covered *wigwams* of the Algonkian, the Iroquois had rectangular bark lodges, called long houses. These they arranged inside their stockaded villages in regular rows, like streets inside a walled town. But many customs were common to both the Iroquois and their Algonkian neighbors. One of these was the practice of using *wampum* (white, purple, or black beads made from shells and woven into a belt) as money. Another was the smoking of a long-stemmed peace pipe as a symbol of agreement at tribal councils.

Throughout the deep and quiet forests of the east roamed large numbers of deer, bear, beaver, and wildfowl. All the Northeastern Woodsmen hunted these animals for food and clothing. Fish were also plentiful in the region's many lakes and rivers, and could easily

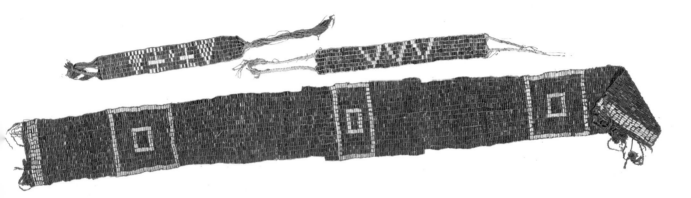

be caught by shooting stone-tipped arrows into the water. Along the Atlantic coast, where cod, flounder, and shellfish abounded, Algonkian fishermen used bone hooks fastened to lines made of milkweed fiber.

But the Algonkians and Iroquois did more than hunt and fish for their food. Outside their villages were well-tilled garden plots—sometimes covering as much as 20 acres—where they grew squash, corn, beans, and pumpkins. To clear these fields, the Indians used the slash-and-burn technique. They would "ring" (cut away a strip of bark around the trunk) the trees so that they would ultimately die and fall. The area would then be burned, and later, crops planted.

Like Indians throughout the American continent, both the Algonkian and the Iroquois believed that the land and its produce, like the

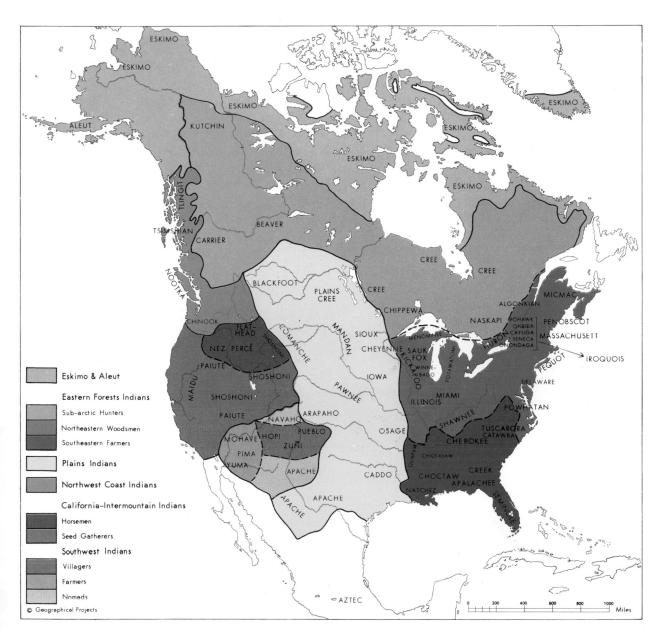

Above: North America, showing the probable location of the more important Indian tribes at the time that Columbus arrived in the New World. North American Indian tribes are generally divided into a number of *culture areas,* or regions in which all the tribes shared about the same *culture* or way of life. These areas are indicated on the map by colors. The regions inhabited by the Aleut and Eskimos, who are not Indians, are also shown.

air and the water, could not be "owned" as personal property. A tribe would claim a certain area as its territory for farming or hunting, but it was held in common by the entire tribe. Again like other American Indians, Northeastern Woodsmen possessed a deep respect and reverence for nature, and believed in supernatural forces that linked human beings to every other living thing. They thought that each animal and tree, each natural element, had its own spirit, and some believed that there was a higher force, or Great Spirit, that shaped and guided all events.

Living close to nature, and believing in its power, the Northeastern Woodsmen strove to live in harmony with it. They sincerely believed that illness, misery, and misfortune would result if that harmony were disrupted. In addition to the chiefs and tribal councils

17

Below: "The Indian Council" by Seth Eastman. Many tribes had the tradition of a tribal council to settle any quarrels within the tribe and decide on a common policy toward outsiders, but the confederation of Iroquois tribes known as the Five Nations was the most highly developed form of all the North American Indian organizations. Women, too, played an important part in tribal affairs. Some, as in Eastman's painting, became chiefs and took part in tribal councils.

that led the tribes, there was always a medicine man, or *shaman,* who was believed to possess special powers. It was his duty to cure the sick, ensure good crops or good hunting, call on supernatural forces for aid against an enemy, and maintain the tribe's harmony with the spirit world.

The Iroquois were among the most warlike Indians on the whole of the American continent. Feuds among the tribes led to frequent raids—for honor, for revenge, or in defense of tribal lands. The Iroquois men carried spears and tomahawks as well as bows and

arrows, and often wore a single long "scalp lock" over the top and down the back of their otherwise shaven heads to taunt their enemies. Intertribal wars were generally limited by mutually-accepted rules, but enemies were scalped, burned, or slaughtered without remorse. To the Iroquois, pain and death were regarded as a test of courage, and those unfortunate enough to be captured often died singing or whistling in order to prove their bravery. Scalping was a ritual of warfare. The victim could be alive, unconscious, or dead, it did not matter. The scalp—a strip of skin torn from the crown of the head—was a battle token, to be displayed with pride in the scalp dances that followed victory.

The Huron Indians of southern Ontario and the Iroquois of New York were frequently at war. About 1570, a Huron refugee named Dekanawidah and the Mohawk Indian chief, Hiawatha, persuaded the chiefs of five Iroquois tribes—the Mohawk, Seneca, Oneida, Cayuga, and Onondaga—to unite themselves in a tribal federation. He urged them to renounce war, at least among themselves, and to present a united front against any other tribe outside this federation, or league, which was to be called the Five Nations. In preparing the code of the confederacy, its creator stated: "I, Dekanawidah, and the chiefs of the tribes in this League, now uproot the tallest pine tree and into the cavity left in the earth we cast all weapons of war. We bury them from sight, deep in the ground, and plant again the tree. Thus shall the great peace be established."

The chiefs and elders of the Five Nations met each summer at the largest village of the Onondaga, near what is now the city of Syracuse in New York state. Fifty peace chiefs, selected by the mothers of the leading families in each tribe, made up the central council. Certain women chiefs also had a place in this council, where issues were discussed and decided by vote. Each tribe had only one vote, and difficult problems were debated until a solution agreeable to all could be found and approved unanimously.

The Five Nations—which became the Six Nations when the

Tuscarora Indians of North Carolina joined them later on—was able only rarely to unite all its members against a common enemy. Nevertheless, it did succeed in ending the conflicts among its member nations, and was, both in theory and in practice, the most highly developed Indian union north of Mexico. Despite the ravages and turmoil that came to the region with the advent of the white man, the league remained unbroken for over 200 years. Ultimately, its democratic principles and structure may have shaped the ideals of the men who created the United States Constitution.

Above: one of the constructions of the Hopewell people—a serpent mound in Ohio. Although by the time the white men arrived the Hopewell Indians had given way to other people in the Ohio River Valley that had once been the center of their remarkable culture, these huge ceremonial animal-shaped mounds and the dome-shaped burial mounds stand as a reminder of their accomplishments.

Below Tennessee and North Carolina, in the region that we now call the Deep South, lived the third major group of Eastern Forests Indians: the Southeastern Farmers. These included the Tuscarora, Creek, Apalachee, and Seminole of the South Atlantic coast; the Cherokee of Tennessee; and the Quapaw, Chickasaw, and Choctaw in the lower Mississippi Valley.

Many of the southeastern tribes practiced a distinctive way of life developed by a group of mound-building Indians in the lower Mississippi River Valley. These, the so-called Mississippian Indians, had begun flourishing about A.D. 1000, and had swiftly developed a strong, agriculturally-based society composed of village-states. The Mississippians possessed a complex religious system, and built their communities around special religious centers—large, earthen mounds topped with wooden temples—where their leaders conducted elaborate rites and ceremonies.

By the time the white men came in large numbers, the Mississippi Valley culture had begun to decline. This was possibly as a result of the epidemics of European diseases that originated from the white men, wiping out large numbers of the Indian people before they even met the explorers. As late as the 1600's, however, small groups of these people could still be found. One of the surviving groups was the Natchez Indians, some 6,000 of whom were discovered by French explorers in 1682. They lived in nine towns along the Mississippi River. Ruled by a single, despotic leader who was believed to be descended from the sun, the Natchez were strictly divided into classes, or castes, ranging from the "Great Sun" and all his relatives

Below: feuds and wars between Indian tribes were frequent, but within the tribe, around the common fire, life was generally ordered and tranquil. Here Indians in Virginia gather to celebrate a victory around their fire.

at the top, to the "Stinkards," or common people, at the bottom.

Not all the farming people of the Southeast adhered as strictly to the old Mississippian way of life as the Natchez, however. In Georgia and Alabama, the mound-building Creek tribes had established a more democratic unity in the form of a loose confederacy of almost 50 towns divided into two categories: the Red (warrior) towns, and the White (peace-keeping) towns. And in southern Florida and the Keys, where farming was unknown, each of the various tribes proudly went its own way.

Wherever farming was done in the Southeast, corn was the primary crop. From it the Indians made corn soup, hominy (corn mash), and flour for the loaves of bread that they baked over the fire

Sioux Indians of the plains playing a form of lacrosse, as painted by Seth Eastman around 1847. The Sioux were one of the tribal groups whose pattern of life was most changed by the coming of the white men. Then they acquired horses and guns, which made it possible for them to hunt buffalo with such skill and efficiency that the vast herds of the western prairies were dwindling long before the white men came onto the plains to join the hunt.

and sometimes "buttered" with bear fat. Wild cane—in thickets called cane-brakes—also grew abundantly in the fertile soil of the southern river valleys. The Indians used sharply cut stalks from the brakes to spear single fish, or drew cane baskets across the rivers to catch dozens of fish in one sweep.

West of the Mississippi River, in the broad expanse of prairie that stretched from the Mississippi River to the Rocky Mountains, and from Canada's Saskatchewan River to central Texas, dwelt the hard-riding, buffalo-hunting Plains Indians. Perhaps it is they who have left behind the most enduring image of the American Indian. But surprisingly enough, the colorful and exciting way of life we think of as so characteristic of the Plains Indians came about

23

chiefly as a result of the Europeans' entry into North America.

For at least 1,000 years before the coming of the white man, large numbers of the Plains tribes had been farming peoples, living in semipermanent villages of earthen lodges. Among these tribes were the Osage in Missouri, the Mandan in the Dakotas, and the Caddo in eastern Texas. These Indians supplemented their diet of home-grown food with buffalo meat, but did not make buffalo-hunting their way of life.

The tribes whose existence did center around the buffalo lived in

Above: George Catlin painted this scene of a Sioux buffalo chase in 1832. He described the Sioux tribesmen as "a bold and desperate set of horsemen." Left: a 1703 drawing showing Indians hunting "beeves," or buffalo, as they did before the arrival of the horse. The European artist obviously imagined buffalo would look like ordinary cattle.

the more westerly regions of the Plains. Among these tribes were the Blackfoot of southern Canada; the Comanche and Arapaho of Wyoming and Colorado; and the Apache of Texas. These nomadic tribesmen followed in the wake of the immense herds of shaggy bison that roamed the prairies. They lived in cone-shaped *tepees* covered with painted buffalo hide, and transported their belongings by means of *travois* (two-poled frames with a bundle suspended between them) originally drawn by dogs, and later by horses. They hunted single buffaloes by creeping up on them dressed in animal skins, and sometimes killed large numbers of them at one time by stampeding them over a cliff. When they killed more animals than they needed right away, they preserved some of the meat in the form of *pemmican,* a combination of dried and pounded beef mixed with hot fat. Berries were added to give it flavor. In common with other North American Indians, the men wore buckskin breechcloths,

leggings, and moccasins, while the women wore leather skirts or dresses. Chiefs well-known for their bravery had the right to adorn themselves with tall feathered war bonnets.

The way of life of the western Plains Indians came to be adopted by all the peoples of the prairie lands when they acquired two prized European possessions: the horse and the gun. Horses had inhabited North America in prehistoric times, but became extinct on the continent during the Ice Age. They were reintroduced by the Spanish explorers and colonists who came to the Southwest in the mid-1500's and early 1600's. Although at first the Spaniards tried to prevent the local tribes from learning how to handle their horses, the Indians soon taught themselves to ride them. And it was not long before raids on the Spaniards' Southwest ranchlands, and trading among the tribes spread the animals throughout the Plains.

Meanwhile, firearms had begun appearing among the Plains tribes to the north. Originally given to the tribes of the Northeast by French and English traders, guns quickly passed westward from tribe to tribe, reaching the Plains Indians before the white man did.

By the late 1700's, both guns and horses were in wide use by the Indians of the grasslands. Increasing numbers of tribes moved into the area—Cheyenne and Sioux from the east, Comanche from the west, Blackfoot from the north, and Pawnee from the south. Some

An American Indian man and woman eating together, drawn by John White. He reported that the Indians were "very sober in their eating and drinking." In fact many tribes lived on the perilous edge of starvation. When hunting was good and food was plentiful, they ate richly, but a hard winter left them struggling to survive.

25

were fleeing from the encroachments of the white men to the east. Others were drawn by the dynamic and profitable way of life then in full swing on the Plains. Horses and firearms greatly facilitated bison hunting and the nomadic pattern of existence that went with it. Often many tribes would meet for a communal hunt. At such gatherings there would be games, foot and horse races, and intertribal council meetings. Sometimes as many as 20 different language groups would gather together, communicating with one another by a sign language of hand gestures.

The acquisition of horses and firearms increased the restlessness and aggressiveness of the Plains tribes. Tribal warfare—for glory, captives, horses, or revenge—became more and more common. But the object of a war was never mutual slaughter. Often the fighting would break off after the first casualties. And one of the most highly honored battle exploits was to touch a live enemy without harming him, and get away safely.

West of the Plains Indians, beyond the Rocky Mountains and along the Pacific coastline from southern Alaska to northern California, lived another major group, the Northwest Coast Indians.

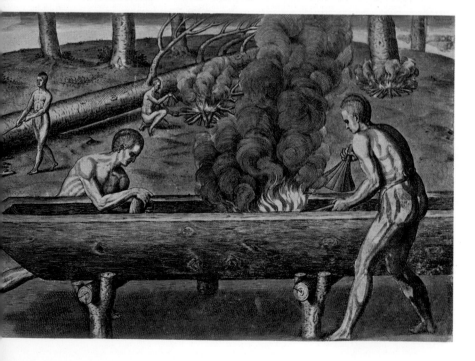

Left: the tribes dependent on fishing from rivers and lakes became adept canoe-builders. Some made light birchbark canoes; others, such as the Indians in the Virginia region shown here, used fire to fell and hollow out tree trunks.

Right: Canadian Indians making music, from a history of America published in Paris in 1722. Music with chanting and dancing was part of many rituals. Below: the Sioux bear dance, by George Catlin. Prospective hunters would dance for several days before the hunt, with songs to the Bear Spirit. The dance was led by the chief medicineman, dressed as a bear, and the dancers—some wearing bears' heads—would circle, imitating a bear to the accompaniment of drums.

Among them were the Tsimshian, Tlingit, Nootka, and Chinook. In this region of misty mountains and rushing streams, farming was unknown, but salmon, halibut, cod, and shellfish abounded. Life was relatively easy here, and the Northwest Indians had time and leisure to develop arts and crafts. They made ornamental wooden masks, built gabled plank houses, and carved lofty wooden poles, called *totems,* which they stood outside their doors. Totem poles depicted their owners' guardian animal spirits, and symbolized wealth and prestige. The Indians of this area were, in fact, inordinately concerned with wealth and social status, and devoted much of their time to making and acquiring possessions. To demonstrate his riches, a man of property would hold a feast or celebration called a

27

The Southwest Indians, living in a hot, dry climate, developed a high degree of cooperation in their societies, working together to bring water to their crops, and living together in city-like pueblos, such as the cliff dwelling here, Montezuma's Castle National Monument in Arizona.

potlatch, in which he would ostentatiously give away or destroy his possessions. As he freed his captives, distributed his household goods, and burned his house down, he would sing boastful songs about himself and make fun of his rivals. A man rich enough to hold a series of potlatches became known as a noble.

In California, and in the area of plateaus and deserts between the Rockies and the Sierra Nevada, lived the Indians who are collectively called the California-Intermountain Indians. But the Indians of this region followed different ways of life. The Paiute and southern Shoshoni of Nevada and the Maidu of California, for example, were Seed Gatherers. They lived a nomadic life, gathering various kinds of seeds, nuts, and berries as they ripened. The seed-gathering tribes were loosely organized, but possessed a rigid social code. Many, for example, practiced an intricate system that required a man who had injured the property, person, or feelings of another to recompense him with an elaborately worked out payment for damages. In common with many other tribes, the Indians of California were fond of making music. They played flutes, eagle-bone whistles, and rattles, and used halves of large hollow logs placed over a pit to form drums upon which they danced out the rhythm of their songs.

Another group of western tribes, called the Horsemen, are also classed among the California-Intermountain Indians. The Horsemen tribes, most notably the Nez Percé, Flathead, and northern Shoshoni, combined some of the ways of the seed gatherers with a number of customs—like riding and buffalo-hunting—that they had learned from the Plains Indians.

Of all the North American tribes, few possessed as stable and highly developed a culture as the Southwest Indians. Here, in the region noted for its canyons, deserts, and high, rocky mesas, dwelt the peoples who, more than any other Indian group, were to be successful in retaining their identity and way of life after the coming of the white man.

Despite the aridity of the region, the people of the Southwest began farming almost 2,500 years ago. Using irrigation techniques that by A.D. 600 had developed into vast networks of canals, they were able to obtain enough water for their large plots of corn, cotton, squash, and beans. By about A.D. 700, one of these farming groups, the Pueblo (from the Spanish word for "village") had begun building large many-storied dwellings in northern Arizona, New Mexico, Utah, and

Colorado. About A.D. 1000, they began to build their homes on the tops of mesas, or in the arched hollows of cliffsides. About A.D. 1300, something—perhaps a drought or increased enemy attacks—caused many of the cliff dwellers to abandon their homes and settle farther south, near the Zuñi and the Hopi in Arizona and New Mexico. Together, these three groups are known as Villagers.

When the first Spanish explorers arrived in the region, they found the Pueblo Indians following a complex way of life in compact communities of multistory buildings. Each village was an autonomous political unit ruled by a council of advisers, and all decisions were made on the basis of what was best for the group as a whole. Religion played an important part in the life of the community, and the men spent a large part of their time engaged in elaborate and regular ceremonial rites.

Like all the American Indians, the peoples of the Southwest reared their children with the utmost gentleness. But unlike other Indian groups, they took care to instill in their offspring an abhorrence of all violence, aggression, and competitiveness. Indeed, the Pueblo, Zuñi, and Hopi were the most peace-loving and orderly of all the American tribes. Conservative, even conformist in temperament, they took a commonsense approach to life. Marriage, for example, was a practical arrangement, and could be ended by the wife whenever she chose. She simply put her husband's belongings outside the door, and he went back to his own family.

Another group of southwestern tribes, called Farmers, lived a less complicated existence than the Hopi, Zuñi, and Pueblo Indians. Although they, too, grew crops, these tribes—the Yuma, Pima, and Mohave of Arizona—moved about more than the Villagers, and dwelt in big houses built of brush and dirt.

Still another group of tribes, the Nomads, included the Navaho and Apache Indians who first began moving into the Southwest from the Northwest around A.D. 1000. Fierce warriors, the Apache carried out frequent raids on the peaceful desert dwellers for captives, horses,

Above: the interior of a Cree Indian tent, drawn in 1820. A forest people, the Cree were hunters and fishers, continually on the move through the woods of North America. Their tents, like the rest of their possessions, were therefore necessarily portable.

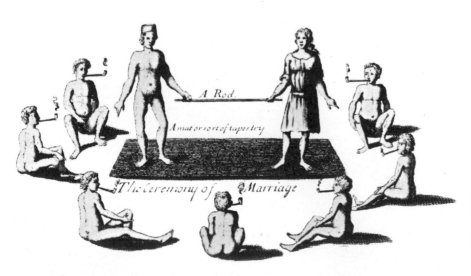

Left: "The Ceremony of Marriage", as imagined through European eyes, from an account of American life written by Baron de Lahontan, at one time the lord-lieutenant of Newfoundland. He wrote his book as a series of letters from Canada between 1684 and 1687.

and other booty. The Navaho, on the other hand, came to stay. Living in cone-shaped *hogans* made from poles covered with earth, they gradually adapted to the ways of the Hopi, Zuñi, and Pueblo.

Far, far to the north of the desert dwellers, in the Arctic regions of Canada, lived a very different group of people, the Eskimo and Aleut, descendants of the last waves of migrating peoples from Asia. Living in skin-covered tents in summer, snow-banked igloos in winter, these hardy people were skilled hunters and fishermen, who had developed a wide variety of bone and ivory tools to help them in their struggle for survival. One of their most ingenious inventions was the *kayak*, a one-man canoe consisting of a light wooden or bone frame covered with tightly sewn skins. The rigorous demands of the cold, white world they lived in made the Eskimo and Aleut a tough and independent people, although family life in their isolated clan groups was warm and easygoing.

Above: an Eskimo hunting, showing him in his kayak. From the Arctic wastes inhabited by the Eskimo, to the tropical heat in which the Mayan Empire flourished, the inhabitants of the two continents skillfully adapted themselves to their different environments.

There could be no greater contrast to the Eskimos' self-reliant way of life than the highly regimented existence of the Indians of Latin America. Here, at the time of the Spaniards' arrival in the 1500's, there flourished two mighty empires—the Aztec of Mexico, and the Inca of South America. Militaristic and expansionist in outlook, both empires were founded on a strong agricultural base. The peoples of each lived in sophisticated urban centers and possessed elements of culture that rivaled many of the developments of the Old World. Their magnificent temples, their elaborate road and irrigation networks, their achievements in mathematics and astronomy (which echoed the even more brilliant Mayan culture that was then on the decline), and their elaborate religious and political systems, continue to astonish modern archaeologists and historians.

But in the 1500's it was something else about the two great Indian

Above: Chac-Mool, the Mayan Rain
God, a statue in the Temple of the
Warriors, Chichén Itza, Yucatan, dating
from about 1300. He holds a dish
awaiting the sacrifice of human hearts.

empires that impressed the Spaniards: the immense hoards of Aztec
and Inca gold. And it was the search for yet more gold that led
the Spaniards to begin exploring the American South and Southwest
in the early 1500's. Meanwhile, not to be outdone by the Spanish,
French and English ships began scouring the north Atlantic coast in
search of a passage to the riches of the East.

All these activities sprang directly from Columbus' first fateful
voyage to the New World in the autumn of 1492. But the tribes who
lay asleep there in the early hours of October 12 could not know or
imagine the events that lay ahead. Dreaming, perhaps, of corn
rustling in the wind, of flashing salmon, or of stampeding herds of
bison, the Indians of America slept on in the forests and grasslands,
the rainy mountains, and wind-swept deserts, unaware that with the
dawn would come the start of a dramatic and shattering new era.

The Lure of Gold

2

Spain was swift to exploit Columbus' spectacular find in the western Atlantic. Now was her chance to challenge Portugal's long and aggravating monopoly on exploration, trade, and treasure. For almost a century, Spain had looked on as Portugal's daring navigators worked their way down the west coast of Africa, forging the first links in an eastern sea route to the Orient. The Portuguese had secured exclusive trading rights wherever they had stopped along the way, and it was clear that they would do the same when they reached the Eastern lands of spice and treasure.

But now, with Columbus' momentous discovery, Spain, too, had a claim to make and defend. In 1494, Spain's King Ferdinand V and Queen Isabella, with the aid and support of the pope, made an agreement with Portugal that safeguarded Spanish rights in the western Atlantic. According to this agreement—called the Treaty of Tordesillas—an imaginary north-south line was drawn 370 leagues west of the Cape Verde Islands, dividing the unexplored regions of the world into two equal halves. Portugal was given the rights to all lands east of that line (including the eastern bulge of Brazil). Spain was granted the rights to all lands west of it.

In effect, Spain had been given almost the whole of the New World, though, of course, at that time she did not know that it *was* the New World, or that it encompassed two vast continents. None-

Left: the Spanish passion for gold first bewildered and then embittered the Indians whom they interrogated, enslaved, and murdered during their relentless search for the precious metal. Here in a drawing of the 1600's Indians take their revenge—pouring molten gold down the throats of the Spaniards, "throwing their greed at them with these words; 'Eat gold, eat gold, insatiable Christians.'"

Right: a gold pendant of the 1400's, representing the Aztec god of the dead, Mictlantecuhtli. A remnant of a dead civilization, it is one of the few golden objects still surviving, having escaped being melted down by the rapacious Spanish conquistadores.

A Mexican painting of about 1550, showing the Spanish entering Mexico. The figure in the dark suit without a helmet is Cortes. With him is the famous Moor soldier Estevanico. In spite of the humid climate, the soldiers wore their full armor on ceremonial parade as well as during battles.

theless, she lost no time in calling on her citizens to explore her western claim, to colonize it, convert its heathen peoples, and uncover its wealth. The men who answered this call were the rough and ready *conquistadors,* eager to win fame and fortune through conquest and adventure. Gold had already been found on the island of Hispaniola, where Columbus had established a colony in 1493. Who knew how much more gold might lie elsewhere in these western lands? So the conquistadors swept north, south, and east from Hispaniola, exploring, conquering, colonizing—and always seeking gold.

By 1512, the Spanish had established themselves in Jamaica, Cuba, Puerto Rico, and the Isthmus of Panama, where, in 1513, Vasco Núñez de Balboa first sighted the mighty Pacific. The same year, a 63-year-old Spaniard named Juan Ponce de León, seeking a legendary isle where a magic mountain was said to make old men young again, discovered the Florida peninsula.

Meanwhile, Spanish exploration along the coast of Latin America had turned up some information that was far more tantalizing to the young conquistadors than any mythical "fountain of youth." In 1518, an expedition led by Juan de Grijalva had explored the Mexican coast from Yucatán to what is now Veracruz and come back with stories about a fabulously wealthy people living somewhere in the interior. Within the next three years the truth of these stories became abundantly clear with Hernando Cortes' discovery and conquest of the Aztec. Here at last was the gold and silver Spain had dreamed of. But the treasure of the Aztec was only the beginning. Francisco Pizarro's conquest of most of Peru in 1532 uncovered an even more magnificent hoard of gold and silver—that of the Inca empire. The riches of Mexico and Peru began flowing back to Spain by the shipload, and soon the wealth of the New World was adding some $30 million a year to the coffers of Spain.

But the search for gold and silver did not end with the discovery of the Aztec and Inca. If anything, it intensified. Other conquistadors, their imaginations reeling with dreams of gold and glory,

Right: Pánfilo de Narváez being chained before Cortes, his blinded left eye bandaged. Behind, the soldiers of Cortes assault Narváez' stronghold with cannons. Narváez was held by Cortes for two years before he could escape.

looked to the lands north and east of Mexico as a possible source of further riches. No one had yet found the fabled "Seven Cities of Cibola"—said to be even wealthier than the cities of Mexico and Peru—but every conquistador believed that they existed, and hoped that he might be the one to find them.

One such man was Pánfilo de Narváez, a soldier and explorer who had taken part in the conquest of Cuba in 1511. In 1521, he had been sent by the Cuban governor to arrest Cortes, whose brutal excesses in Mexico had begun to alarm the Spanish authorities. But Cortes had got wind of the mission before Narváez arrived, and met him at Veracruz, where he put out one of his eyes and imprisoned him for two years. When Narváez at last escaped and returned to Spain, he was rewarded by the king with a grant to conquer and establish a colony in Florida.

On June 17, 1527, Narváez sailed from Spain with 5 ships, 600 men, and 100 horses. When the fleet reached the Caribbean, it was struck by a fierce hurricane, in which two ships and scores of men were lost. Frightened by this experience, 140 of the men refused to continue with the expedition, preferring to remain behind in the West Indian colony of Santo Domingo. Undaunted, Narváez collected his remaining men and sailed on to Tampa Bay, halfway along Florida's west coast. From here, in 1528, he decided to proceed by land, taking with him the 42 horses that had survived the voyage, and 300 of his men. He left the others behind to man the ships,

Indians collecting gold in about 1563, as reported by Jacques le Moyne de Morgues who was in Florida with the French at that time. The picture, first published in Frankfort in 1591, was titled "How gold is gathered in the rivers descending from the Appalachian Mountains." The sight was to prove elusive to Narváez and his followers.

with orders to follow the coast and meet him at a point farther north.

One of Narváez' officers, Álvar Núñez Cabeza de Vaca, strongly opposed the idea of splitting up the party and leaving the relative safety of the coast. But Narváez overruled all opposition. He had seen flakes of gold in an abandoned Indian fishing net, and was convinced that the fabulous Seven Cities lay in the interior. Cabeza had no choice but to follow his commander inland.

The men made slow progress as they marched north through Florida's glades and marshlands. All along the way they were sniped at by Indians who had developed a fear of white men because of Spanish slave raids along the coast. Using powerful bows, the Indians shot at Narváez' troops with flint-tipped arrows that went right through the soldiers' armor. But when the mounted Spaniards wheeled and charged their assailants, the Indians simply disappeared

The Florida swamplands, virtually the same as they were when Narváez and his men splashed their way northward. With dwindling supplies and under constant harassment from the Indians, Narváez and his men eventually abandoned their quest for gold.

into the woods. On one occasion, the soldiers did manage to capture an Apalachee chief and questioned him closely about the golden cities they were seeking. But the chief could only tell them that the peoples beyond were much poorer than those of his own region.

Despite these gloomy tidings, Narváez continued to push on through the wilderness. At last, however, dwindling supplies forced him to give up his quest and return to the coast. But he did not find his ships there to meet him. After sailing up and down the Florida coast for many weeks looking in vain for some sign of the expedition, the crews had given up the search and sailed back to Spain. Narváez and his followers found themselves marooned.

Desperate, Narváez ordered his men to start building boats. All the metal that could be spared—from stirrups, spurs, crossbows, and weapons—was forged into nails, saws, and axheads. Trees were felled and planks hammered together to make five crude barges whose seams were caulked with palmetto fiber and pine tree resin. The horses were killed for food and their manes and tails used to make rope. Despite persistent Indian attacks, the men at last finished the makeshift boats, and the 250 weary survivors clambered aboard. "The boats were so crowded that we could not move," wrote Cabeza later. "With the gunwales only six inches above the water, we went into a turbulent sea, with no one among us having a knowledge of navigation."

Helped by the currents, and occasionally by the wind that filled the boats' crude patchwork sails, the little fleet inched its way along the coast under the watchful eyes of the armed Indians on shore. Because they could not land without placing themselves at the mercy of these hostile observers, the Spaniards soon ran short of food. But the worst was yet to come. Sometime after passing the mouth of the Mississippi River, the flotilla was caught in a storm. Narváez' boat was blown out into the Gulf of Mexico and disappeared. Others of the frail craft capsized. A mere 85 exhausted men survived the shipwreck, dragging themselves ashore on the barren coast of southern Texas.

The castaways had escaped with their lives, but nothing else—without food, clothing, tools, or weapons. Too weak to fish, they grubbed for roots and berries. Many of them died in the weeks that followed. Others were taken captive by local tribes who treated them as slaves, kicking, beating, or working them to exhaustion,

"Cabeza de Vaca stranded in the Texas desert," by Frederic Remington. After the shipwreck in which most of his companions were killed, De Vaca was taken captive by an Indian tribe, and was held by them for nearly six years.

MEXICO.

MEXICO. REGIA
ET CELEBRIS
HISPANIÆ NO
VAE CIVITAS

and occasionally killing them at will. Only a few of the Spaniards fell into the hands of friendly Indians. One of these fortunate individuals was Álvar Núñez Cabeza de Vaca. He won the trust and admiration of his captors and ultimately become one of their traders, traveling to other tribes to exchange and acquire articles such as seashells for cutting, ocher for war paint, cane for arrows, sinews for bowstrings, and flint for arrowheads. Cabeza lived among the Indians for nearly six years, sharing with them the frequent hunger and starvation that was part of life in this desolate land. He wrote later that, "Occasionally they kill deer or fish, but the quantity is so small and the famine so great, that they eat spiders and the eggs of ants, worms, lizards, salamanders, snakes, and vipers: they eat earth and wood, the dung of deer, and other things that I omit to mention."

Finally, Cabeza and three other men—among them a Moor named Estevanico—were able to escape from their captors. Heading in the direction of Spanish Mexico, the four struggled through deserts, grasslands, and mountains for many months. At long last, they reached the fringes of a Spanish settlement in Mexico. There, on an April day in 1536, they were sighted by a troop of Spanish cavalry, who stared in amazement at the four exhausted men who were staggering toward them out of the wilderness.

The four were treated as heroes in Mexico City where, according to Cabeza, they found it somewhat difficult to readjust to the trappings of civilization. "I could not wear any [clothes] for some time," he writes, "nor could we sleep anywhere but on the ground."

Cabeza's return to Mexico stirred fresh interest in the regions to the north of Mexico. Though the Indians who had befriended him had themselves been dreadfully poor, they had spoken of rich tribes farther north. When Cabeza reported this, he raised the hopes of those who believed that the Seven Cities of Cibola might still be found. Accordingly, Estevanico, the Moor who had escaped with Cabeza, was sent northward again on a reconnaissance mission, this time in company with a Franciscan priest named Fray Marcos de Niza. When they reached one of the Zuñi settlements in New Mexico, Estevanico somehow managed to offend the community, and was killed. Fray Marcos, however, escaped unharmed, and returned to Mexico City. There, for some unknown reason, he not only confirmed, but exaggerated Cabeza's report of riches to the

The title page decoration from Cabeza de Vaca's book. the rumors he reported of rich Indian tribes living farther north led more men to chance their lives on more expeditions seeking gold.

north. No further encouragement was necessary. The Viceroy of
Mexico set the wheels in motion for a major expedition to find
and capture the wealth of this fabled northern kingdom.

Francisco Vásquez de Coronado was put in charge of the expedi-
tion, which consisted of no fewer than 300 Spanish soldiers and
noblemen and several hundred Indians. Setting out in 1540,
Coronado kept his men at a fast pace, convinced that immense
treasure lay before him. The expedition marched into what is now
Arizona, reaching the Grand Canyon before turning eastward into
New Mexico. Here Coronado discovered the Zuñi pueblo of
Hawaikúh. This, he thought, must be the "silver city" described by
Fray Marcos. He ordered his men to attack. Uttering the traditional

war cry used before a battle with infidels—"Saint James! Spain! blood! fire!"—the Spanish troops stormed the fortress, and at last captured it, along with the stores of food they badly needed. But to their great disappointment, they found no treasure in the pueblo.

But perhaps, Coronado thought, the fabled Seven Cities lay farther on. Still hoping, he pressed on until he came to the Pueblo Indian settlement of Tiguex on the Rio Grande. Here the expedition was granted peaceful entry into the town. Once inside, however, the Spaniards began stripping the blankets off the very backs of the Indians, and fighting broke out. But the Pueblos' war clubs were no match for the Spaniards' muskets and lances, and the Indians were soon defeated. To celebrate the victory, Coronado's captains

Francisco Vásquez de Coronado and his enormous expedition, which started out in 1540. In spite of the numbers of his men, and his ruthlessness in dealing with the Indians, Coronado returned to Mexico in 1542, no more successful than his predecessors.

45

A pottery jug in the shape of an owl, from a Zuñi Indian pueblo. Coronado's men, hoping to find gold, were bitterly disappointed to discover nothing they considered of value in the pueblos they ransacked. They were contemptuous of the men who had mastered the gentle art of molding clay into practical, decorative, everyday objects.

cruelly burned 30 Pueblos at the stake and slaughtered 60 more.

But carnage and pillage had not brought the Spaniards one step closer to the mythical Seven Cities. Coronado led his men as far north as Kansas, all to no avail. The treasure still eluded him. In the course of the journey, he, or members of his party, had explored the Rio Grande River, the Grand Canyon, the Southern Rockies, and the Great Plains. They had traveled farther into the American wilderness than any white men before them. Nevertheless, because they had found no gold, their expedition was held to be a failure and Coronado returned to Mexico in 1542, a ruined man.

While Coronado and his men were marching through the South*west*, a rival expedition, led by Hernando De Soto, was exploring the South*east*. De Soto had taken part in the conquest of Peru in 1532, and his share of the Inca gold had made him so rich that, back in Spain, even the king had borrowed money from him. Spending lavishly and living the life of a Spanish *grandee*, De Soto had become a symbol of the success to be had in the New World.

The grateful king of Spain made Hernando de Soto governor of Cuba and gave him a free hand to explore and conquer Florida. De Soto needed no urging to undertake the task. He believed that Álvar Núñez Cabeza de Vaca had been hiding the truth about the wealth of the peninsula, and he was certain that he would find the legendary Seven Cities there.

As a well-known conquistador, De Soto had little trouble raising an army for his expedition. He had his pick of soldiers, and chose only the fittest men with the best weapons and the finest armor. He bought seven ships, fully equipped, and sailed for the New World. After a stop in Cuba, he set out for Florida, reaching the Tampa Bay area in May, 1539. With him were 600 men, 213 horses, a pack of dogs, and a herd of swine, brought along to provide a continuing food supply.

Soon after the ships landed, Indian smoke signals appeared up and down the coast, warning of the white man's presence. The Indians guessed that De Soto would prove as unpleasant an intruder as any of the other white men who had appeared on their coast. Tragically, they were all too right. De Soto was casually, inhumanly cruel to the Indians he encountered as the expedition marched northward. He hunted them for sport, sometimes throwing them to his dogs to be torn to pieces, or having them beheaded by the

Above: Hernando de Soto. He launched his expedition into the Southeast on a wave of glory generated by his success in Peru. Hoping to repeat the Peruvian triumph, he took a lavishly equipped expedition to Florida in 1539.

Right: De Soto was well-known for his cruelty to Indians even before the expedition into Florida, where all his atrocities did not help him find a single grain of gold. Instead, he found himself in situations such as that pictured here, when Indians, afraid to tell him there was no gold when he demanded to be taken to gold mines, would lead him on long marches. When no gold was to be found, De Soto, enraged, would have their hands cut off.

score to test his men's swordsmanship. When the expedition reached an Indian village, the Spaniards would loot and burn it, torturing the chiefs and massacring the inhabitants. Those they spared were turned into slaves and dragged along behind the soldiers in chains attached to collars around their necks. If they complained, they were burned at the stake, or punished by having their hands cut off.

But this unmitigated cruelty produced no treasure. De Soto found no gold in Florida, nor in Georgia, nor in the Blue Ridge Mountains of North Carolina and South Carolina. The only valuable article he collected was a pearl necklace given to him by a woman chief of one of the Creek tribes along the Savannah River. In the course of the march northward, he met a lone survivor of the ill-fated Narváez expedition, a man called Juan Ortiz, who had been living as a slave of the Indians for almost 10 years. Ortiz had heard no reports of gold and silver. But perhaps, De Soto thought, this was only because the man's captors had kept him in ignorance of

47

Above: those of De Soto's men who decided to stay with the Creek Indians were typical of many Spaniards in the New World. Their children were the first mestizos (mixed Indian/white), now the racial majority in the former Spanish colonies in South America.

the Seven Cities. So De Soto pushed on—minus a few of his men, who had found the land so rich, the life so comfortable, and the Indian girls so attractive that they opted to remain among the tribes of the Creek confederacy in Georgia. Certainly, life among the Indians seemed preferable to the hardships of interminable marches in search of elusive golden cities.

De Soto now turned westward, marching into Tennessee, and then southward into Alabama. Here, some of his soldiers were boldly attacked and put to flight by a band of Indians. Seeing this, the Spaniards' Indian slaves broke free of their captors and ran to

the village of their fellow Indians, who smashed their chains and armed them. In retaliation, De Soto attacked the village in force, killing 2,500 men, women, and children.

At this moment, word reached De Soto that his fleet was waiting for him on the Gulf coast, only six days' march away. But he kept the news a secret from his men. He was not yet ready to leave. He did not want to return empty-handed and lose his reputation. A year of exploration had yielded only a handful of pearls and the loss of scores of men. Without sending word to the waiting ships, he turned northwest, away from the Gulf. In May, 1541, while making

"De Soto at the Mississippi." This painting, by W. H. Powell, shows the Spanish force in vigorous strength. In fact, they arrived at the river exhausted and worn after months of struggling through unknown, difficult territory, beset by hostile Indians.

his way through northern Mississippi, he discovered the great Mississippi River and crossed over it into Arkansas.

Months passed, and De Soto found himself still struggling through deep forests and bayous (small rivers), still fighting Indians, and still looking in vain for the golden cities. At last, in northeastern Louisiana, he returned to the Mississippi River. There, after routing a large force of hostile Indians, De Soto had four large boats built. The expedition floated downstream to the treacherous bogs and bayous of the lower Mississippi Valley where, in 1542, worn out

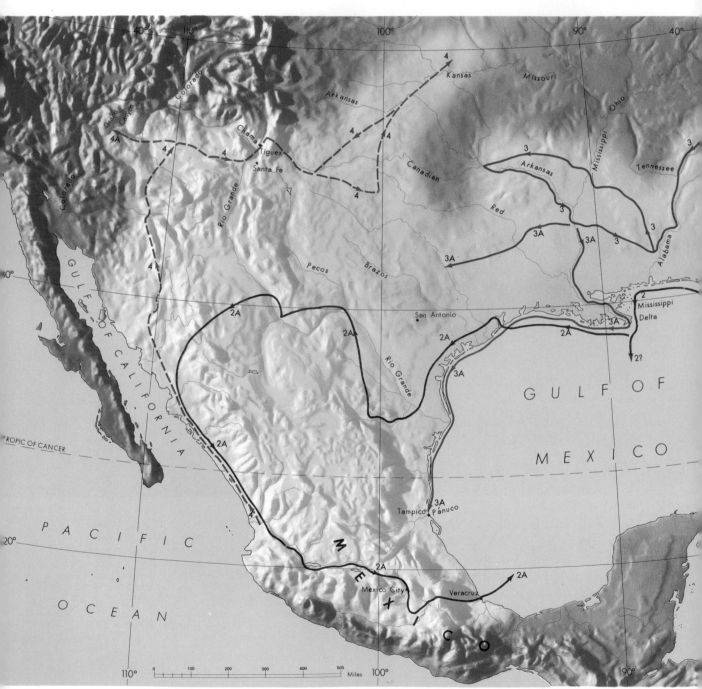

and sick with fever, De Soto died. His men, fearful that the Indians would mutilate the body if they found it, weighted his body with stones and dropped it into the depths of the river during the night.

Before he had died, De Soto had named as his successor a man called Luis de Moscoso. Under his leadership, the expedition briefly explored northeast Texas, finding nothing but impoverished Indians who fled at the sight of the white men. Recognizing the truth of Cabeza's bleak description of these lands, Moscoso retraced his steps to the Mississippi River. Here he decided to build boats

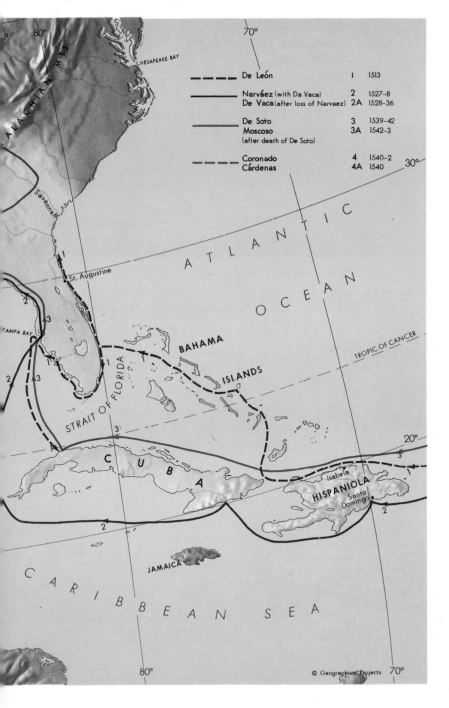

Left: the southern United States and Mexico, showing the routes of the Spanish explorers searching for gold in Mexico and the southern states in the early 1500's.

and sail down the river to the Gulf of Mexico. Using all the available iron—including the chains and collars that had shackled the Indian slaves—the men hammered together seven crude brigantines. The remaining 322 Spaniards set out in these boats in the spring of 1543. Somehow, despite constant Indian attacks, most of them managed to survive the 700-mile journey to the Gulf of Mexico. Then they sailed on until they reached Tampico on the Pánuco River, about 200 miles north of Veracruz. Here they sighted Indians wearing European clothes, and realized that they had reached the safety of Spanish Mexico.

De Soto's expedition had long since been given up for lost, and the Spanish settlers in Mexico stared in wonder at the 300-odd men who had miraculously survived four years in the American wilderness. Nevertheless, the expedition was considered a total failure. No gold or other treasure had been found, and the Indian inhabitants had resisted conquest, so the land could not be brought under the Spanish flag. The only mitigating factor was De Soto's discovery of the Mississippi River. Moscoso's voyage down the great river to the Gulf of Mexico had demonstrated that the Mississippi was a navigable waterway leading directly into the heart of the North American continent.

The expeditions of Narváez, Coronado, and De Soto put an end to Spanish dreams of finding the Seven Cities of Cibola, but Spanish colonial ambitions remained undimmed. Throughout the 1500's, continued efforts were made to secure a Spanish foothold on the

Left: Indians fighting a Spanish force. De Soto's expedition of 1539–42 was under continuous attack by Indians, who had the advantage of knowing the country and quickly learned to use the weapons that they took from the slain Spaniards. The sense of the Indian presence, lurking in the background, must have added to the strain on the surviving men, even when they were not actually being besieged.

Right: a map of Spanish America, from a mariner's atlas with maps of the whole known world, made in Portugal probably in 1573. This map has the Spanish coat of arms to indicate which areas were Spanish possessions.

Atlantic coast, and numerous Jesuit missions were founded from Florida to Chesapeake Bay. The only eastern outposts to endure however, were those in Florida, where the missionaries were able to convert the Apalachee and Calusa and establish a permanent settlement on the east coast at St. Augustine in 1565.

Meanwhile, the Spanish were making plans to colonize the Southwest. Under the leadership of Juan de Oñate, a group of settlers, soldiers, and priests traveled to New Mexico in 1598 and founded a colony at the Pueblo of San Juan de los Caballeros near the Chama River. But the Pueblo Indians they enslaved to work their land rose up against them in 1680, and it took almost 12 years of fighting to reassert Spanish rule. Sante Fe was established as the capital of the Spanish province of New Mexico in 1610, and courageous Spanish missionaries founded outposts throughout the Southwest. But the fierce Apache and other warlike tribes of the Southern Plains prevented the Spanish from extending their rule farther north. The Spanish colonists had more success in Texas, where they founded the Mission of San Antonio de Valero, now called the Alamo, in 1718. And in California, Franciscan missionaries, under the able leadership of Father Junípero Serra, set up no fewer than 21 missions between 1769 and 1823. Among these were San Diego, Santa Clara, San Gabriel, and San Francisco.

But long before Father Junípero built his California missions, the fortunes of Spain had begun to wane. The treasure of Mexico and Peru was not inexhaustible, as the Spaniards found out in the late 1500's, when the golden harvest began to dwindle noticeably. And to make matters worse, French, Dutch, and English pirates had begun waylaying gold-laden Spanish galleons on their way back to Spain. As early as 1526, a French corsair named Jean Fleury had commandeered some of Cortes' treasure ships in mid-Atlantic and sailed home with them to his own king. Despite official Spanish protests, piracy on the high seas rapidly increased in scale during the century. In 1580, the daring English seaman Francis Drake triumphantly returned home in the *Golden Hind* with some $40 million in New World gold and silver taken from Spanish vessels.

And what of the treasure that did reach Spain? Much of it went to finance a series of wars against the French and the Turks. Much of it, too, was squandered by Spain's devout Catholic king, Charles, in a futile effort to stem the tide of Protestantism then sweeping through Spain's holdings in Germany and The Netherlands. Charles vowed he would not spare his "dominions, friends, body, blood, life, or soul" in the fight against heresy. But even his determination was surpassed by that of his son, Philip II, who came to the Spanish throne in 1556.

Philip zealously stepped up his father's crusade against Protestantism on the European continent. But his own particular grievance was against England, where the state religion of Catholicism had been replaced by Protestantism. England's Queen Elizabeth I added insult to this injury by rejecting Philip as a suitor, by aiding the

Right: St. Augustine, Florida, in 1760. The modern city is the remnant of the Spanish attempt to establish an empire on the Atlantic coast. Only in Florida, where the Jesuits converted the Apalchees and Calusas, did they build a permanent settlement.

Right: not only were the treasure ships ripe for pirates swarming over the sea, but Spanish towns found themselves vulnerable. In this engraving French pirates plunder the Spanish town of Chiorera on the island of Cuba in 1556.

Protestant Dutch when they rebelled against their Spanish masters
in 1568, and by actually knighting Francis Drake for his wholesale
robbery of Spanish gold on the high seas. In 1587, the Protestant
queen consented to the execution of her Catholic cousin, Mary,
Queen of Scots. This was the last straw. Philip swore vengeance,
and, in 1588, launched a war fleet—the mighty Armada—to teach
England a lesson. Unfortunately, the lesson was Spain's, for almost
the entire Armada was vanquished by a combination of English
naval power and a severe storm at sea.

By now, Spain's treasury was almost empty and the country

deeply in debt. No further major efforts of conquest could be made in the New World. Missionary work and colonization continued, particularly in South America, where Spanish plantation owners, often mercilessly exploiting the native population, ruled with an iron hand. But over her vast northern claims, Spain could exert little or no control. Helpless to defend her interests there, she was forced to stand aside while the explorers, traders, and colonists of other nations strode through her forests, sailed up her rivers, and established mastery over lands whose real riches the Spanish conquistadors had never even dreamed of.

Above: the English launch fireships against the Spanish Armada anchored at night off the coast of Calais in August, 1588. The defeat and destruction of the Armada was a severe blow to the power of Spain. The riches of the New World — taken at such a price in both Indian and Spanish lives — were dwindling, and the most that Spain could do was develop the areas that were already conquered.

Seeking the Northwest Passage

3

Early in the 1500's, the Treaty of Tordesillas became a thorn in the side of King Francis I of France. It seemed grossly unfair to him that a mere piece of parchment should give Spain and Portugal exclusive rights to all the world's newly discovered lands. Soon after coming to the throne in 1515, Francis wrote a scathing letter to the King of Spain saying, "Show me, I pray you, the will of our father Adam, that I may see if he has really made you and the king of Portugal his universal heirs."

As if to add fuel to Francis' envy and frustration, Spain proceeded to top Portugal's control over Eastern spice and treasure with her own conquest of the glittering Aztec empire in 1521. This was too much for the French king to bear. Treaty or no treaty, he declared, he would break his southern neighbors' unjust monopoly over trade and treasure. He would send explorers of his own to find and claim the western sea route to the Orient.

From about 1504, French fishermen had been sailing into the North Atlantic Ocean to fish for cod in the Grand Banks off the coast of Newfoundland, and rumor had it that somewhere along that coast there was a strait that led to China. If Francis' mariners could locate that strait, then France, too, could enter the inter-

Left: a map of Canada drawn by a Portuguese cartographer before 1547. (North is at the bottom: to orient the map turn it upside down.) The map shows Cartier, but it is disputed whether it shows him leaving France or arriving in Canada with his settlers.

Right: "Francis I of France," painted by Titian in about 1536. It was he who challenged the pope's division of the newly discovered lands between the Spanish and Portuguese crowns.

national race for riches. Accordingly, in 1524, Francis sent a highly skilled Italian navigator named Giovanni da Verrazano to seek out this fabled "Northwest Passage."

Verrazano followed a somewhat southwesterly course and may have reached the shores of North Carolina. Then he sailed north along the New England coast, reaching Newfoundland before returning to France. Historians believe that in the course of the voyage, he spent some time near the mouth of the Hudson River, which he later described to the king as being "very large and pleasant." He went on to report that, "We greatly regretted having to leave this region, which seemed so delightful and which we supposed must also contain great riches."

King Francis was pleased with Verrazano's report. The voyage, though it had failed to produce any significant information about the much-desired strait, did allow the king to make certain grandiose claims to the region Verrazano had explored, and it was not long before the northeast coast of the mysterious northern continent was being referred to as "New France."

Wars in Europe forced Francis to abandon his quest for the Northwest Passage for almost 10 years. Then, in 1533, he received a petition from one Jacques Cartier, proposing a new exploratory voyage to the American coast. Cartier, born in the French town of St. Malo, had sailed and fished in the waters of the North Atlantic, and had spent a few adventurous years as a corsair, pirating Spanish vessels. Inspired by reports of Verrazano's voyage, he was now eager to try his hand at finding the fabled shortcut to China. Francis willingly granted Cartier's request, and in 1534 outfitted him with two small vessels and a crew of 120 men.

Cartier reached Newfoundland after 20 days at sea, and made a brief stop at tiny Funk Island to replenish the ships' larder with the murres, gannets, and great auks that abounded there. The men soon found that they were not the only hunters on this rocky "Island of Birds." Cartier noted in his journal that "although the island is 30 miles from the mainland, bears swim there to eat the birds, and our men found one as large as a cow and as white as a swan, swimming as swiftly as we could sail."

Leaving Funk Island, Cartier's ships sailed up and around the northern tip of Newfoundland and passed through the Strait of Belle Isle into the Gulf of St. Lawrence. Rounding the eastern tip

Above: the Gulf of St. Lawrence, with Percé Rock on the Gaspé Peninsula. Neither Verrazano, nor Cartier on his first voyage, recognized the importance of the gulf as the opening to the sea of one of America's greatest waterways.

Left: a glazed terra-cotta bust, by an unidentified Italian artist, of Giovanni da Verrazano, the mariner who probably discovered the mouth of the Hudson River, where New York City now stands.

of Anticosti Island, the vessels crossed the gulf—completely missing the mouth of the St. Lawrence River—and anchored off Gaspé Peninsula. Suddenly, as they lay at anchor there, Cartier saw a fleet of 50 birchbark canoes approaching them, bearing Indians who began "making signs of joy as if desiring our friendship and saying in their tongue *napeu tondamen assurtah*." This was the Micmac Indians' phrase for "we wish to have your friendship."

The next day the Micmac returned, holding up furs as a sign that they wished to trade. Cartier obliged by giving them some knives and a red hat for their chief. When the Frenchmen went ashore, they were greeted by the other men and women of the tribe. The women sang and danced, "rubbing our arms with their hands, then lifting them up to heaven and showing signs of gladness." In exchange for the white men's knives, hatchets, and beads, the Indians traded every pelt they had—even to the furs they were wearing—"until they had nothing but their naked bodies."

Above: Jacques Cartier. He had gained his early sailing experience fishing in the North Atlantic. It was due to his navigational skill that his three ships were able to sail some 800 miles up the uncharted St. Lawrence River.

Before leaving Gaspé Peninsula, Cartier and his men erected a 30-foot cross and fixed to it a shield bearing the French emblem, the fleur-de-lis. Below the shield they printed in large bold letters the words "LONG LIVE THE KING OF FRANCE!" Then, while the puzzled Micmac stood gazing at this monument to an unknown faith, king, and country, Cartier took two captives, young braves named Domagaia and Taignagny.

In his report to King Francis, Cartier included the information—learned from his captives—that there was a great river leading westward from the gulf he had discovered. Could this be the Northwest Passage? To find out, Francis commissioned Cartier to make a second voyage, this time with three vessels. So, on May 16, 1535, Jacques Cartier set out once more for the New World. With him on the flagship *Grand Hermina* went Domagaia and Taignagny, to serve as interpreters.

Again Cartier passed through the Strait of Belle Isle. But this time he continued westward until he reached the mouth of the great river. He named it the "St. Lawrence," because he first saw it on August 10, St. Lawrence's feast day. He sailed up the St. Lawrence to the Huron village of Stadacona, near the site of present-day Quebec City. The Huron leader, Donnacona, was called the chief of "Canada" (the Indian name for that part of the St. Lawrence Valley). At first, Donnacona welcomed Cartier with ceremonial

orations and other signs of friendship. But then the chief's attitude abruptly changed. Domagaia and Taignagny, no doubt bitter about their year of captivity, had taken Donnacona aside and warned him not to let the white men proceed any farther up the river.

But how was the chief to prevent them? Donnacona tried sending three of his braves dressed in black and white dog skins, with blackened faces and horns on their heads, to frighten the white men. But the wild shrieks of the Indian "devils" only made Cartier's men laugh. Donnacona threatened and pleaded with Cartier to no avail. On September 19, the Frenchmen hoisted sail on the ship's pinnace (tender) and sailed up the St. Lawrence, leaving Domagaia and Taignagny behind at Stadacona.

After traveling 150 miles up the river, they came to the Indian village of Hochelaga. Here they were met by 1,000 men, women and children, who gave them a joyful welcome and provided them with a feast of fish and cornbread. When darkness fell, the sailors returned to their boats, while the Indians continued dancing and singing around the great bonfires they had lighted to celebrate their arrival.

Early the next morning, Cartier and some of his men were taken on a tour of the village. The Algonkian, believing Cartier to be a medicine man, brought all their sick and wounded to him to be healed. Even their chief, an old man shaking with palsy, was carried

Below: Jacques Cartier erecting the cross at the entrance to the Gaspé harbor, as painted by Samuel Hawksett. With the cross, Cartier claimed the newly discovered territory for France.

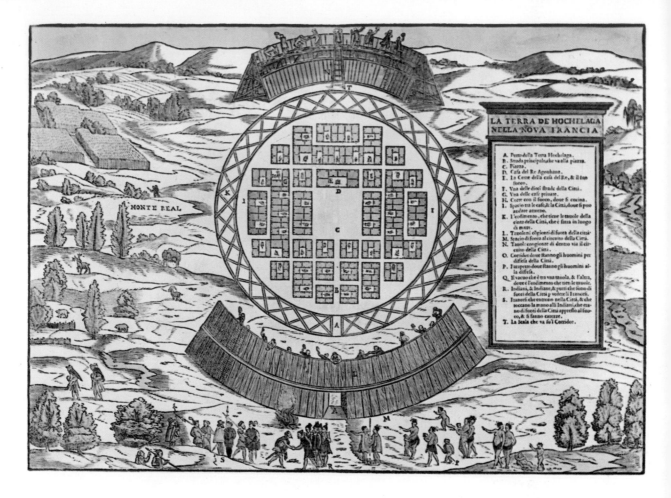

MONTE REAL

LA TERRA DE HOCHELAGA
NELLA NOVA FRANCIA

A. Porto della Terra Hochelaga.
B. Strada principale che va alla piazza.
C. Piazza.
D. La Corte del Re Agouhanna.
E. La Corte della casa del Re, & il suo fuoco.
F. Una delle dieci strade della Città.
G. Una delle case private.
H. Cuore con il fuoco, dove si cucina.
I. Spatio tra le case, & la Città, dove si può andare attorno.
K. L'andimento, che tiene le tauole della cinta della Città, che è fatta in luogo di mura.
L. Tauoleni di giontí di fuora della città.
M. Spatio di fuora al circuito della Città.
N. Tauole congionte di dentro via il circuito della Città.
O. Corridor doue stanno gli huomini per difesa della Città.
P. Parapetto doue stanno gli huomini alla difesa.
Q. Il vacuo che è tra una tauola, & l'altra, doue è l'andimento che tien le tauole.
R. Indiani, & Indiane, & parti che sono di fuori della Città a vedere li Francesi.
S. Francesi che entrono nella Città, & che toccano le mano alli Indiani, che erano di fuori della Città appresso al fuoco, & si fanno carezze.
T. La Scala che va sù'l Corridor.

to Cartier on the shoulders of 10 braves. But the French captain resisted the temptation to play healer, and instead solemnly opened his Bible and read out to the bewildered populace a passage from the Gospel of St. John.

Cartier and his men then climbed the mountain that rose high above Hochelaga. It was almost sunset, and the forests he could see for 60 miles around were ablaze with autumn colors. Cartier was enthralled by the view from the summit of this peak, which he named Mont Réal (Mount Royal). The city, Montreal, takes its name from the mountain. To the southeast, over the shining ribbon of the St. Lawrence, he could make out broad, fertile valleys and the Green Mountains of Vermont, "a country," he wrote later, "which is the loveliest a man could see." But to the west he saw a series of swift rapids churning up the river a short distance beyond the point where he had anchored. The Indians told him that there were still more rapids beyond these. This was disheartening news, for it destroyed Cartier's hopes of using the St. Lawrence as a waterway to the East. With bitter irony, he named the foaming waters "Sault La Chine" (or Lachine)—the Chinese Rapids.

Cartier then sailed back down the St. Lawrence to Stadacona, where he decided to spend the winter. It proved a grim experience,

Above: the plan of the Indian village of Hochelaga, on the site of Montreal. The earliest known picture of the place, it comes from a book published in Venice in 1565. The rapids that prevented Cartier from going farther west were just beyond the village.

for he and his men fell prey to scurvy, a vitamin-deficiency disease. They became weak, with swollen joints, shrunken sinews, and rotting gums. At one point there were only three men strong enough to bring food and water to the entire ship's company. Fearful that the Indians would attack them if they knew their weakness, the feeble men forced themselves to make noise and look active whenever the Indians drew near. Twenty-five men died before Cartier learned by accident from his one-time captive Domagaia about a cure for the disease—a potion made from the boiled bark of the white pine, which contains vitamin C.

When at last the winter ended, Cartier returned to France to report his findings to the king. Although he had not found a

Above: "A View of the City of Montreal, taken from the top of the Mountain, the 15th October 1784," a watercolor by James Peachey. The mountain is Mont Royal, which Jacques Cartier named.

Below: the modern city of Montreal. as viewed from Mont Royal. The Indian village that Cartier found has become an internationally important city and a vital symbol of the French contribution to present-day Canada.

Above: Cartier and his followers in Canada, from a manuscript map by Pierra Desceliers, drawn either in 1536 or 1542. It is possibly the only contemporary and authentic picture of Cartier. This is only a section of the map, which shows the whole world.

Left: the detail showing Cartier.

navigable waterway to the East, Cartier, like his sovereign, continued to believe in its existence. There was no doubt in either man's mind that it would be found. The only question was when, and by whom? Cartier himself made another voyage to Canada in 1541. Again, he sailed up the St. Lawrence and again failed to locate the fabled waterway to the East.

French ambitions to find and claim the Northwest Passage were baulked during the late 1500's by a series of bloody civil wars between the French Huguenots (Calvinists) and the French Roman Catholics. Until this internal conflict was finally resolved in 1593, nothing more could be done about exploring New France.

Meanwhile, a lucrative trade in furs had been started by the French fishermen who sailed yearly to the Grand Banks off the coast of Newfoundland. The coastal Indians, they discovered, were only too eager to part with their rich pelts for such things as beads, guns, or whiskey. And back in France, the furs fetched a handsome price. The profit to be made from beaver pelts was particularly high, because at that time beaver hats were in fashion everywhere in Europe. By the late 1500's, this fur trade had become so obviously profitable that other Frenchmen were anxious to cash in on it. At the same time, the French authorities were beginning to think seriously about planting colonies in New France to strengthen their claims there. As a result, the king took to granting individual men short-term monopolies on the St. Lawrence fur trade in return for their promise to settle a certain number of colonists there. But the Laurentian monopoly-holders were always more interested in fur trading than in colonizing, and one grant after another was revoked when they failed to keep their bargain. In fact, the 1600's might have seen little French progress in North America had it not been for the Herculean efforts of one remarkable man—Samuel de Champlain.

Above left: Samuel de Champlain, 1567?–1635. He was responsible for establishing the French in North America, proving with his unquenchable enthusiasm that it was possible for French settlers to live in the American wilderness.

Above: astrolabe used by de Champlain during his exploration of North America. The astrolabe is an instrument for measuring the altitude of heavenly bodies, from which latitude can be calculated. It was replaced by the sextant in the 1700's.

Champlain had grown up an ardent Catholic in the little French harbor village of Brouage. Prompted by a love of adventure, he had accompanied his uncle, an officer in the Spanish navy, to the port of Cádiz in 1598, and soon after had entered the service of the King of Spain. As captain of a Spanish vessel, he had toured the West Indies and sailed along the coast of Central America for two years. On his return he had written an account of his travels for his own king, Henry IV of France. Included in his report were some 60 detailed maps of the Spanish colonies, and an ingenious suggestion for a canal across the Isthmus of Panama.

King Henry was grateful for the young captain's loyalty and impressed by his skill in mapmaking. To reward Champlain, he made him his Royal Geographer, granted him a small pension, and gave him a noble title. But after spending two years at the French court, Champlain became restless again, and when an opportunity for travel presented itself in 1603, he seized it gladly. That opportunity was a chance to serve as official geographer on an expedition to New France.

The expedition, sponsored by the man who possessed the current monopoly on the Laurentian fur trade, sailed from France in 1603. When the party's two ships reached the North Atlantic, they sailed directly up the St. Lawrence River to the site of Hochelaga. But the Indian village visited and described by Jacques Cartier in 1535 had vanished. The Algonkian who once lived there had long since fled to escape the ravages of the aggressive Iroquois to the south.

In the course of charting the region, Champlain encountered several groups of nomadic Indians and from them learned about the existence of a great waterfall to the south—Niagara Falls. Champlain and his comrades traded for furs with these Indians and, when the expedition returned to France in September, 1603, their ships were heavily laden with a valuable cargo of pelts.

In 1604, Champlain sailed again to New France, this time in company with Pierre du Guast, Sieur de Monts, a French explorer who had secured the fur-trading rights along the North Atlantic

Above: an Indian war party landing in a canoe, while Champlain was exploring the New England coast in what is now Massachusetts. It was on this journey that Champlain succeeded in mapping the whole eastern coast of North America from Nova Scotia to Cape Cod.

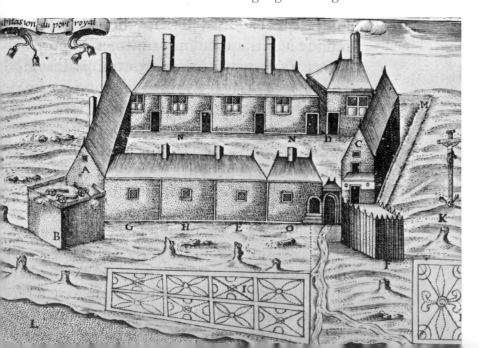

Left: the Habitation of Port Royal, from Champlain's book published in 1613. It was here that the French colonists came after the first grim winter in Nova Scotia's Bay of Fundy.

coast on condition that he settle 100 colonists in the region. Again, Champlain's assignment was to serve as the expedition's official geographer and chartmaker.

Sieur de Monts, Champlain, and the party of colonists chose to settle on the island of St. Croix near the mouth of the St. Croix River in Acadia. But the French flag they raised so bravely in the little settlement on June 25, 1604, came down again sadly the following spring. Winter in Acadia, as the French then called the Nova Scotia area, had been a harrowing ordeal and many had died. The survivors —Champlain among them—moved in 1605 to Port Royal, a harbor on the Nova Scotia side of the Bay of Fundy. The next winter proved so "mild" that only a quarter of the people died—a blessing, considering the usual death rate in the New World colonies of this period.

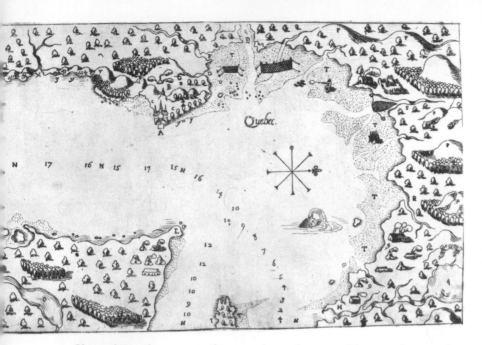

Champlain then set off to explore the coastline to the south. Passing Mount Desert Island and Penobscot Bay, he reached the site of present-day Portland, Maine, where he noted that "large mountains are to be seen to the west"—the White Mountains of New Hampshire. He then proceeded south to Massachusetts Bay, where he explored the mouth of the Charles River, site of present-day Boston. Continuing along the coast, he visited Plymouth harbor—where some 15 years later, the Mayflower would land its band of Pilgrims—and explored the bay side of Cape Cod's long crooked arm. Then, in 1607, having explored and mapped the entire North Atlantic Coast from Nova Scotia to Cape Cod, Champlain sailed back to Port Royal, and from there returned to France.

The next year, he was back in New France, this time as Sieur de Monts' representative in the Laurentian region. Sieur de Monts had just been granted the fur-trading monopoly there, and wished to establish a trading post at a strategic location along the St. Lawrence River. Accordingly, Champlain led a small expedition up the river to a place not far from the old Huron village of Stadacona. Here he ordered that a fort, a warehouse, and three small huts be erected. On July 3, 1608, the trading post was officially opened. It was called Quebec.

Champlain was convinced that the St. Lawrence would one day prove to be more than a convenient fur-trading route. He believed that the legendary Northwest Passage branched off from it somewhere, and that little Quebec would become famous as the first stopping point on the fabled water route to the Orient. He could not guess that Quebec's future greatness would rest, instead, on its being a cornerstone of the Canadian nation

From the first, however, Champlain realized the value of maintaining good relations with the local Indians. Only with their help

Above left: a map of Quebec and the surrounding area, from a book by Samuel de Champlain published in 1613. This is the first picture of Quebec.

Above: "A View of the City of Quebec the capital of Canada taken from the Ferry House on the Opposite side of the River, October 3rd, 1784," an aquatint painted by James Peachey.

Right: the skyline of modern Quebec at sunset, photographed by M. Milne. Sited spectacularly on the St. Lawrence River, Quebec is one of the world's most beautiful and elegant cities.

could the French hope to acquire pelts from the interior. Early on, Champlain won the confidence of the region's Huron and Algonkian tribes. He got on well with the proud and eloquent Huron braves, and relished the company of the comfort-loving Algonkian. Soon Quebec became the object of regular visits from Indian fur traders, and in the fall of 1608, Champlain sent some of his men back to France with a heavy cargo of pelts. He and 28 others remained behind to man the fort at Quebec.

In the spring, a group of Huron braves came to Champlain and

begged his assistance in a raid they were planning against their Iroquois enemies to the south. Rashly, Champlain agreed to help them. Taking two of his own men, he set off with the war party in early summer. In birchbark canoes, the group paddled west along the St. Lawrence River and then, after a journey through the thick woods, traveled south via the Richelieu River to the lovely lake which now bears Champlain's name. Here, near the site of what would one day be Fort Ticonderoga, the party met a group of Iroquois braves paddling along the shore. A canoe from either side cautiously advanced and drew together for a brief discussion.

Right: Zacherie Vincent, a Huron brave, in a self-portrait. Born in 1812, he described himself as the last of the full-blooded Hurons.

Above: Champlain firing his arquebus at Iroquois Indians. The French were to pay dearly for Champlain's quick decision to help the Huron warriors. Not only were the French settlements along the St. Lawrence River constantly harried by raids, but also the Iroquois eventually joined forces with the English in their wars with the French.

Because dusk was falling, it was agreed to begin the fight the next day. Both sides spent the night in warlike song and dance, loudly defying each other.

With the dawn, the adversaries joined battle. Facing Champlain's companions were 200 Iroquois warriors. The Huron had kept the three white men hidden until the very last moment. Then, as the early morning mist cleared, the Iroquois suddenly saw Champlain, clad in gleaming armor, stride forward and take his place at the head of the Huron braves. Champlain describes what happened next: "When I was within 20 paces, the enemy, halting, gazed at me; as I also gazed at them. When I saw them move to shoot I drew a bead on one of the chiefs. I had loaded with four bullets and hit three men at the first discharge, killing two on the spot. When our Indians saw this they roared so loudly that you could not have heard it thunder. Then arrows flew like hail on both sides. But when my companions fired from the woods, the Iroquois, seeing their chiefs killed, turned tail and fled."

It was a glorious moment for Champlain and his Huron friends. But in later years, his siding with the Hurons against the Iroquois turned out to have been a grave tactical error. Once the Iroquois learned that their enemy's white allies were Frenchmen, they never

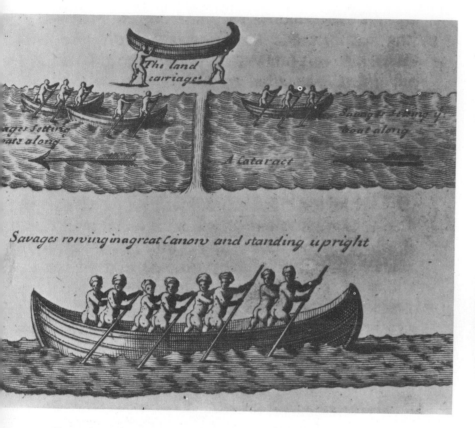

Savages rowing in a great Canow and standing upright

The land carriage

A Cataract

Above: an early drawing of Canadian Indians with their canoes, published in 1703. It was supposed to demonstrate the method of portaging and paddling the canoes. In fact, the painting by Cornelius Krieghoff, opposite, is based on more accurate observation.

forgot it. Nursing their grudge against the French, they launched countless raids on subsequent French settlements along the St. Lawrence. Ultimately, the Iroquois joined forces with the British, and played a vital role in the struggle that won Canada for Britain in the 1700's.

Before Champlain returned to France in 1610, he persuaded the Algonkian to take a young French boy, Étienne Brulé, with them to their winter home west of Hochelaga, so that he might learn more about the region. The plan worked well, for when Champlain returned in the spring of 1611, Brulé was able to describe to him a route west over the Ottawa River to a great lake, the Huron. Champlain was anxious to follow up this lead, but he was prevented from doing so by trouble in Quebec. Sieur de Monts had lost his monopoly on the Laurentian fur trade, and a motley crew of greedy men had come over from France to make a quick profit in beaver pelts. These rough opportunists were hard to control, and the

brandy they brought with them as a trading commodity made the Indians equally wild. Champlain had to use all his diplomatic skill to keep the peace. In desperation, he returned to France to try to obtain some authority over the region. There, he finally persuaded a French nobleman to act as viceroy for the region, with Champlain himself as lieutenant governor.

Returning to Canada in 1613, Champlain found that most of the Huron Indians had left the St. Lawrence region. Two thousand braves had waited in vain for him in 1612. Their disappointment at his failure to return, plus the traders' brandy and treachery, had driven them back into the interior. All of Champlain's painstaking Indian diplomacy had been unraveled.

But at this moment, he met Nicholas Vigneau, a Frenchman who claimed to have found the water route from the St. Lawrence to the sea. Champlain accepted this fantastic story at face value, and immediately set off up the St. Lawrence to see for himself. After a

Above: an 1858 painting by Cornelius Krieghoff showing Indians portaging furs. In the Canadian wilderness, where most of the rivers were fast and shallow, with large numbers of rapids, any long-distance travel was likely to involve a succession of these portages.

75

calamitous journey up the Ottawa River, during which he almost drowned in the churning rapids, Champlain reached an Indian village whose chief soon exposed the unreality of Vigneau's story. Discouraged, Champlain began the long trip back, slowed by difficult portages through mosquito-infested country and dense forests. Only the 60 canoes loaded with furs that followed him downriver to the trading post saved the expedition from being a complete loss.

Champlain returned to France once more in 1614, and sailed back to Canada the following year with a number of missionaries of the Franciscan order. He hoped that the missionaries would help to pacify the Indians as well as keep the peace among the unruly traders. On his return he found that his Indian friends were once more begging for help against the Iroquois, who had now crossed the St. Lawrence and were boldly ambushing the Algonkian along the lower reaches of the Ottawa River. Champlain decided to set

Below: the French employing siege techniques against an Iroquois fort. This was the battle that took place near Lake Oneida, to the northeast of present-day Syracuse, New York.

out and enlist the aid of more distant tribes against the Iroquois.

His search for Indian allies led Champlain to discover important new territories. Following the Ottawa River for some 300 miles, his expedition crossed by portage to Lake Nipissing, then continued southwest to Lake Huron's Georgian Bay. By so doing, Champlain and his men forged a northern water route to the Great Lakes, a route that was to be used by French traders and settlers for decades to come. After paddling the length of Georgian Bay, the expedition traveled to the eastern end of Lake Ontario, and then proceeded

Above: a storm over Georgian Bay, Ontario. It was this bay that the French crossed on the expedition into Iroquois territory near Lake Oneida.

Right: the Great Lakes, showing the routes taken by Cartier, Champlain, and other French explorers in the century between 1534 and 1634. These enterprising men penetrated deep into the heart of the North American continent, along the waters and shores of the St. Lawrence River and the lakes themselves.

south into Iroquois territory near Lake Oneida. There Champlain's band of Indian warriors launched an attack on an Onondaga fort but, despite Champlain's shouted directions and European tactics, they failed to take it. Champlain himself was wounded twice and had to be carried from the scene of battle by his braves. Because the Iroquois controlled all southern approaches to the St. Lawrence, the defeated French and Indians were forced to take the long way back to their homes, via Lake Ontario, Lake Huron, Lake Nipissing, and the Ottawa River.

Champlain wanted desperately to learn more about the region west of Lake Huron, and in about 1620 he sent his young friend Étienne Brulé to explore it. Brulé traveled as far as the Upper Michigan Peninsula—becoming the first white man to visit the area. Champlain himself, however, was prevented from making any

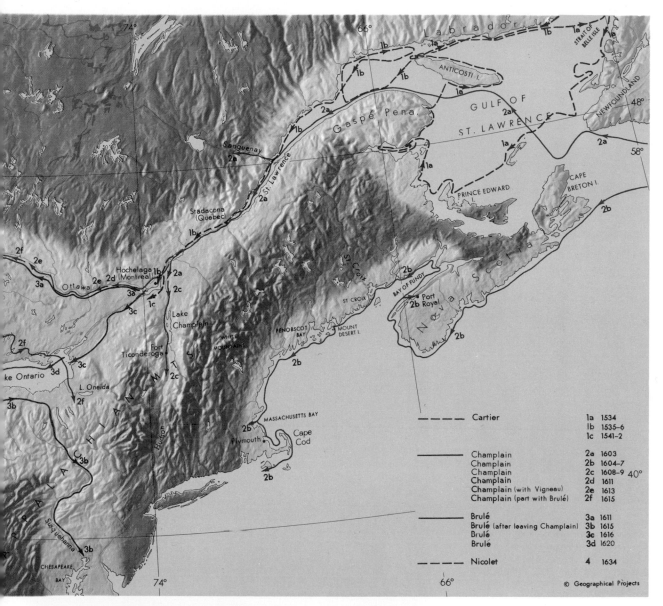

——————	Cartier	1a	1534
		1b	1535-6
		1c	1541-2
—————	Champlain	2a	1603
	Champlain	2b	1604-7
	Champlain	2c	1608-9
	Champlain	2d	1611
	Champlain (with Vigneau)	2e	1613
	Champlain (part with Brulé)	2f	1615
—————	Brulé	3a	1611
	Brulé (after leaving Champlain)	3b	1615
	Brulé	3c	1616
	Brulé	3d	1620
– – – –	Nicolet	4	1634

© Geographical Projects

Left: the arrival of Champlain's wife in Canada. She arrived July 2, 1620, after a voyage of almost two months. For some time Champlain's family and the family of Louis Hébert were the only permanent settlers in Quebec.

further journeys of exploration by his duties in Quebec. He was determined to build up the size and strength of the colony. But, although the fur business continued to flourish, the traders came and went, anxious to make their profit and return to the comforts of their native land as quickly as possible. In the early 1620's, Quebec had only two families of permanent settlers. One was Champlain's own (he had brought his wife over in 1620). The other was the family of one Louis Hébert, a Parisian druggist who in 1617 had gladly seized the opportunity to own his own land in the New World. But

Above: David Kirke taking Quebec, after a siege of the city that lasted for several months of the winter of 1628–29. Champlain had finally been forced to surrender to the English.

Right: Jean Nicolet's landfall on the shore of Lake Michigan in 1634, by E. W. Deming. Nicolet was the *coureur de bois* who was probably sent by Champlain to find out if there was a "sweetwater sea" beyond Lake Huron as had been reported to him. Nicolet, who put on a Chinese robe in honor of the "Asians" he expected to meet, found only Winnebago Indians.

back in Europe, the traders' reports about the hard Canadian winters and the ferocity of the neighboring Iroquois tribes discouraged other Frenchmen from following Hébert's example. Among the other 80-odd souls who dwelt in New France at this time were the dedicated Catholic missionaries who had come over in the service of their faith.

War broke out between France and England in 1627. The French authorities, realizing that the English in North America would probably use the pretext of war to attack New France, dispatched a

fleet of colonists and supplies to strengthen Quebec in 1629. But it was already too late. Before the fleet could reach its destination, it was captured in the St. Lawrence by David Kirke, a Scots merchant-pirate in the employ of England. Rightly guessing that Quebec could not last out the winter without fresh supplies, he sailed up the river and demanded the colony's surrender. Champlain refused, believing that the French supply fleet was on its way. For several winter months, Kirke played a waiting game, living comfortably off the French provisions while the people of Quebec slowly starved. Eventually, Champlain was forced to surrender, and Kirke's 150 men took over the colony. Champlain was taken to England as a prisoner, where he waited out what he was sure would be a conquest of short duration. His prediction was borne out in 1632 when, with the cessation of hostilities between the two countries, Quebec was restored to France.

Back in Canada once more, Champlain worked hard to rebuild the fort and buildings of Quebec. At the same time he sought to repair the alliances with the Indians engaged in the fur trade. Quebec began to grow again under Champlain's guiding hand, and the little fortress became firmly established as an outpost of French civilization in the Laurentian wilderness.

About this time, a new type of adventurer began to flourish in New France. This was the "forest runner," or *coureur de bois*. Drawn as much by the mystery of the virgin hinterlands as by the profits to be made from the fur trade, the coureurs de bois were young men with a taste for solitary adventure and a readiness to adopt the Indians' self-reliant way of life. Preferring the challenge of the wilderness to the comforts of civilization, they roamed far and wide through the Canadian forests gathering furs from the Indians.

It was to one of these coureurs de bois, Jean Nicolet, that Champlain turned in 1634 when he sought confirmation of reports about the great "sweetwater sea" beyond Lake Huron. It was his hope that, from this sea, a waterway to Asia could be found. Nicolet had heard tales of a certain tribe, living on the shores of this sea, who had flat faces and yellow skin. Surely, Champlain thought, these must be the people of the Orient. Accordingly, he equipped Nicolet with a Chinese robe, so that the young man might make a favorable impression when he met these "Asians."

Nicolet probably set out in 1634, traveling up the Ottawa River and overland to Lake Huron. He is believed to have paddled along the north shore of the Lake, and to have passed through the Strait of Mackinac into Lake Michigan. When he reached the clay cliffs of Green Bay, Wisconsin, he thought that he had found the mainland of China. He landed, donned his silken robes, and fired two pistol shots. But, when he scrambled to the top of the cliffs, he found only the Winnebago Indians. These were the "people of the sea" he had been told of! Although Nicolet was very disappointed, he made friends with the Winnebago, who entertained him royally. Then, after traveling a short distance inland via the Fox River, he made his

Above: the statue of Jean Nicolet at Green Bay, Wisconsin. When Nicolet saw the clay cliffs of Green Bay, he thought that he had reached China.

way back to Quebec to report his findings to Champlain. Alas, when
he reached the settlement, he found it in mourning. The great
"Father of New France" had died, on Christmas Day, 1635.

Champlain had devoted his life to establishing the French in
North America. His dauntless energy, sweeping vision, and persistent efforts had enabled him to rise above the greed of his fur-trading
patrons and gain a substantial foothold for France in the New World.
All the storms of life—and there were certainly storms ahead for
the French-Canadians—could never remove the stamp of French
civilization he had imprinted on the St. Lawrence Valley.

Right: Henry VII of England, who gave John Cabot a license for his voyage in 1497 seeking a way to the East Indies. Below: the arrival of the English in Virginia. Thomas Hariot, in his 1590 account, *A briefe and true report of the new found land of Virginia,* wrote of their reception ,"[The inhabitants] brought us to their village in the island called Roanoac and unto their Weroans or Prince, which entertained us with reasonable courtesy, although they were amazed at the first sight of us."

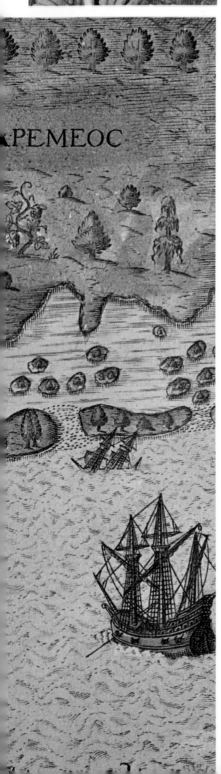

PEMEOC

The English Venture West

England was a step behind France and Spain in the exploration of North America. English mariners did not really begin probing the east coast of the great continent until the late 1500's—almost half a century after the exploits of Cartier, Narváez, and De Soto. Yet, curiously enough, the English flag had been planted on American soil before the banners of either France or Spain.

In 1497, a full 27 years before Verrazano set off to find the Northwest Passage for France, another Italian, one Giovanni Cabotto, had gone in search of it for England. Cabotto had emigrated to England as a young man and, after changing his name to John Cabot, had become a captain for the Merchant-Venturers of Bristol. It was with their backing—and a special license from King Henry VII— that Cabot, no doubt inspired by Columbus' voyages, set out to find the East Indies in 1497.

In a little ship called the *Matthew,* Cabot made his first landfall on the coast of Newfoundland or Nova Scotia. There he landed and, believing that he had reached an outpost of Asia, unfurled the royal standard and claimed the region for the King of England. Then, after sailing around Newfoundland, he returned to England with news of its rich fishing grounds.

But the English king was not pleased with the results of the voyage. Cabot had brought back no spices, no treasure, no emissary from the Great Khan of China—nothing, in fact, to prove that he had reached the East. Henry VII granted Cabot a small pension for his efforts, but warned him that if he intended to make any further voyages westward, he would do so without a royal blessing.

Cabot was undeterred. Apparently, like Columbus, he was convinced that a further voyage would bring him to his goal. In 1498 he set out once more, this time with four or five ships. Again he traveled west, possibly sailing north as far as Greenland and south as far as North Carolina. His own ship went down during a storm on the return voyage, and the crews of the remaining vessels could give only sketchy accounts of the southern coasts they had seen.

Cabot's voyages had given England nothing but a flimsy legal claim to the area he had explored, and English interest in the New World remained almost nonexistent for the next 78 years. England was concerned with other, more pressing matters during this period. At home, the nation was wracked by political and religious strife. And abroad, England was embroiled in conflicts with France and Spain. Meanwhile, English sailors such as Francis Drake—with the blessing of Queen Elizabeth herself—remorselessly plundered Spanish treasure ships on the high seas, an activity that only served to heighten the mounting hostility between the two countries.

Ultimately, it was the conflict and rivalry with Spain that led England to take a fresh interest in the New World. In the late 1500's, a number of Englishmen began urging the queen to carry the battle against Spain to the New World. An English settlement there, they argued, would not only serve as a base from which to launch

Left: Elizabeth I of England, in the portrait by Nicholas Hilliard. During her reign Sir Francis Drake made his great voyages, and enriched not only himself but his queen with the gold snatched from Spanish treasure ships. The ermine on the queen's sleeve is a symbol of virginity, alluding to Elizabeth's popular title "Virgin Queen."

attacks on Spanish holdings in the Americas, but would also act as a check on further Spanish expansion in North America. And, they added, who could tell what riches might lie north of Spain's current holdings on the continent? An outpost in America might one day provide England with vital raw materials, even treasure.

Two of the men who argued for such a colony were Humphrey Gilbert and his half brother Walter Raleigh (or Ralegh, as he spelled it). Both were firmly convinced of the strategic value of an English base in North America. But no individual could simply set off and

establish a colony at will. A charter granting royal permission had to be obtained first. In 1576, 1577, and 1578, an English navigator named Martin Frobisher had received the queen's permission to make voyages in search of the Northwest Passage—voyages which had taken him to Greenland, Labrador, Baffin Island, and Hudson Strait. In 1578, Humphrey Gilbert, following Frobisher's example, petitioned the queen for permission to seek "a passage by the north to go to Cathay." But Gilbert's charter also provided for the founding of a settlement, whose colonists were to have the "privileges of free denizens and persons native of England."

Gilbert set out for the New World in 1578. But his ships were beset by storms in mid-Atlantic, and he was forced to return to England. In 1583, he made a second attempt, and this time succeeded in reaching Newfoundland, which he claimed for Elizabeth I. He set up a colony there, near St. John's, and then sailed for home. But on the return voyage his ship went down in a storm. And the little colony in Newfoundland soon had to be abandoned.

After Gilbert's death, the royal patent was transferred to Raleigh, who was given the right to "discover, search, find out, and view such remote, heathen, and barbarous lands, countries, and territories not actually in possession of any Christian prince." Like Gilbert, Raleigh was granted permission to establish a colony in these lands. But unlike Gilbert, Raleigh dreamed of something more than a mere strategic base in the New World. He wanted nothing less than to found a new England, an overseas empire where English homes,

Above: the French explorer René de Laudonnière with Chief Athore standing before a decorated column at the mouth of the St. Johns River, Florida, 1564. This is the only surviving painting by Jacques le Moyne de Morgues, who was on the expedition. This view of "the land of plenty" is said to have given Sir Walter Raleigh the idea of establishing a colony in America. Below: Sir Walter Raleigh, 1552–1618.

English speech, English culture, and English law might prevail.

In 1584, Raleigh equipped and sent out two ships on a reconnaissance mission to the shores of America. Sailing west-southwest, the vessels reached the sandy beaches of North Carolina, then followed the coast north to Cape Hatteras. They entered Pamlico Sound, and came to an island that the Indians called Roanoke. The island's inhabitants gave the sailors a royal welcome. Arthur Barlowe, who, with Philip Amadas, was in charge of the expedition, later reported that the chief's wife "cheerfully came running out to meet us and commanded her people to pull our boats ashore. When we arrived at her house, she sat us down by the fire, took off our clothes, and washed and dried them. . . .She herself dressed meat for us, and brought us venison, fish, melons, and wine mixed with ginger. . . .We were entertained with all love and kindness and found the people most gentle, loving, faithful, and free of guile and treason, living in the manner of the golden age."

Barlowe's report to Raleigh also included a glowing account of the beauty of the countryside, with its tall trees, wild vineyards, and abundant deer, rabbits, and birds. Raleigh was delighted, and named the newly-found land "Virginia," in honor of the "Virgin Queen," Elizabeth I. Elizabeth, too, was pleased, and knighted Raleigh, instructing him to inscribe his coat of arms with the legend "Walter Ralegh, Lord and Governor of Virginia." In 1585, Raleigh dispatched a second expedition to Virginia. This expedition, led by Sir Richard Grenville, carried colonists. But the little settlement on Roanoke Island fared badly. The colonists, desperately short of provisions, almost starved to death waiting for their meager crops to ripen. The next year, when Sir Francis Drake's fleet made a stop at the outpost, the settlers gladly accepted his offer to take them back to England.

Raleigh's last and most serious attempt to establish a colony in Virginia was launched in 1587, when he sent 117 settlers to Roanoke under the leadership of John White. Soon after the passengers had landed and chosen a site for their settlement, White's daughter, Ellinor Dare, gave birth to a daughter. The infant was named "Virginia," as she was the first English child to be born in America. White's orders were to sail back for additional supplies, and, when he set off, his daughter and her husband, together with little Virginia, were among the 91 men, 17 women, and 10 children left at Roanoke.

The naval battle with the Spanish Armada took place soon after White reached England, and it was three years before he could return to Roanoke. Alas, when he did finally reach the island in 1590, he found it deserted. No trace of his family or their fellow-colonists remained, save for the word "Croatoan" the name of a neighboring island, carved on a tree. Friendly Indians in the region suggested that all the settlers had been massacred on the orders of Chief Powhatan, leader of the confederacy of Powhatan tribes along the coast.

In 1603, a few months after James I became king of England, Sir

Above: the wife and child of an Indian chief in Virginia in about 1585, a watercolor drawing by John White. He was the leader of the Roanoke colony and the grandfather of Virginia Dare, the first white child to be born there.

Above: a map of Virginia drawn by John Smith and published in 1624. In the upper left hand corner is a picture of Powhatan in state. Although called Chief Powhatan by his tribes, his name was actually Wahunsonacock.

Right: an idyllic view of the pastimes a knight could enjoy in Virginia, from an account of 1619. Although hunting and fishing were certainly part of the life in the new colonies, this picture does not reveal that they were less practiced as sports than as a matter-of-fact way of providing food to eat. This kind of propaganda may have been part of the reason that recruits to the colonies found real life in Virginia so desperately hard.

Walter Raleigh was suspected of treason, charged, and imprisoned in the Tower of London. There he remained for 12 long years. But Raleigh's dream of a Virginia colony did not languish there with him. In 1606, the English merchants who had helped finance Raleigh's efforts formed a colonizing association of their own, and were granted the colonial privileges previously enjoyed by Raleigh. The association, called the Virginia Company, was divided into two groups. The Virginia Company of Plymouth (or Plymouth Company) was to colonize the northern portion of the Atlantic coast (from Maine to Maryland), while the Virginia Company of London (or London Company) was to colonize an overlapping section of the mid-Atlantic coastline (from New York to the Carolinas).

In December, 1606, the Virginia Company of London dispatched its first expedition to the New World. Aboard the *Susan Constant,* the *Goodspeed,* and the *Discovery* were about 100 colonists. Among them was one Captain John Smith, a remarkable man who was later to play a vital role in the fledgling colony's fight for survival against the ravages of hostile Indians, starvation, disease, and sheer despair.

John Smith was no stranger to hardship and danger when he set out for Virginia at the age of 26. Indeed, he was already a past master at the difficult art of survival among alien people in alien lands. At 15 he had begun traveling through Europe seeking challenge and excitement, and he had found it in abundance—as a mercenary soldier in the armies of The Netherlands, France, and Hungary, as a slave of the Turks in Constantinople, and as a prisoner of the Tartars in Russia. Romance and adventure had been part and parcel of his life for almost 10 years when he finally escaped from his Russian master and returned to England in 1604. But his wanderlust was still unsatisfied, and when he learned of the Virginia undertaking, he signed on at once.

Before the ships set sail, the London Company had secretly selected six men to serve as the colony's governing council. The list of names was placed in a locked box that was not to be opened until

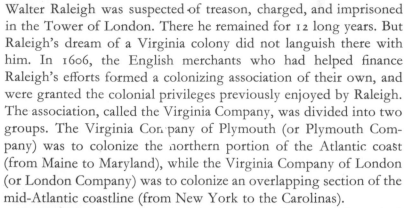

Left: long before John Smith came to America he had proved himself capable of surviving desperate situations triumphantly. Here he is shown in one of the episodes from his early career when he took on three Turkish knights in single-handed combat and defeated each of them in turn. The illustrations come from his book *The True Travels, Adventures, and Observations of Captaine Ione Smith, In Europe, Asia, Affrica, and America,* which was published in London in 1630.

Right: the coat of arms that Smith was awarded after his victory. It shows the heads of the three knights.

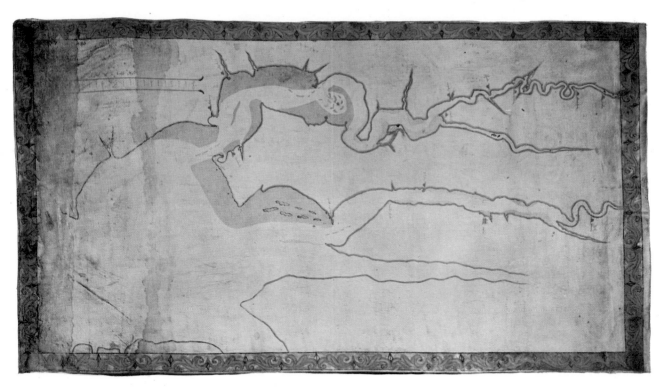

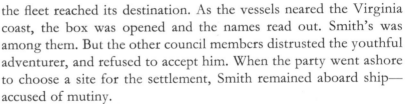

Above: the James River, a vellum map drawn by "Robarte Tindall of Virginia, anno 1608." The colonists dispatched by the Virginia Company of London established their settlement, Jamestown, about 60 miles up the river.

the fleet reached its destination. As the vessels neared the Virginia coast, the box was opened and the names read out. Smith's was among them. But the other council members distrusted the youthful adventurer, and refused to accept him. When the party went ashore to choose a site for the settlement, Smith remained aboard ship—accused of mutiny.

The London Company had specified that the colony was to be built on good land, and in a location that might easily be defended against Indian attacks. These conditions were hardly fulfilled by the site chosen: a mosquito-infested strip of swampland 60 miles up the James River in the very heart of Powhatan country. Here, amid the little cluster of rude dwellings they called "Jamestown," the colonists laid out garden plots under the direction of Edwin Maria Wingfield, the president of the council. John Smith urged Wingfield to put up a fort of wooden logs like those he had seen in Russia, but the president insisted that a mere brushwood fence would serve to keep out the Indians. But, soon after the fence was built, 400 Powhatan braves attacked the settlement, breached the flimsy fortifications, and wounded many men before being frightened away by cannon shot. Wingfield had learned his lesson. Captain John Smith was admitted to the council and a wooden fort was built under his guidance.

But the colony did not prosper. Three months after its founding, 46 men were dead from starvation, malaria, pneumonia, and dysentery, and those alive were so weak that they barely had strength enough to bury the dead. In desperation, the council turned to John Smith, begging him to go out and trade for food with the Indians.

How they tooke him prisoner
in the Ooze. 1607

C.Smith bindeth a saluage to his arme,
fighteth with the King of Pamaunkee and
all his company, and slew 3 of them.

Their   triumph about him

C:Smith bound to a tree to be shott to death
1607

Above left: Captain John Smith being
taken prisoner by Powhatan Indians.

Left: the Indians triumph at Smith's
capture, from his 1624 book. He had
gone up the James River hunting food
for the colony, hoping to trade with the
Indians. When he went ashore, he
found himself surrounded by warriors.

Ætatis suæ 21. A°. 1616.

...toaks als Rebecka daughter to the mighty Prince Powhatan Emperour of Attanoughkomouck als Virginia converted and baptized in the Christian faith, and Wife to the wor.ll M.r Tho: Rolff.

King Powhatan comands C. Smith to be slayne, his daughter Pokahontas beggs his life his thankfullnes and how he subiected 39 of their kings. reade ye history

Smith made his way along the James River. When he had traveled about 50 miles, he suddenly found himself confronted by 200 Powhatan warriors. After a brief skirmish, Smith was taken prisoner. But he was cunning as well as brave, and managed to convert their hostility into curiosity—first by writing a letter to the council at Jamestown, and then by showing them his compass. The magic of the "talking paper" and the little needle under the clear "ice" that always pointed in the same direction gave him a reputation as a medicine man. He was taken to the Powhatan's leader, Wahunsonacock, known to his tribes as Chief Powhatan. There, in the presence of the great chief and all his council, Smith's fate was debated. At last, after much deliberation, it was decided that the white man should die, and Smith was forced to put his head between two large stones so that the warriors could beat out his brains with their clubs. But at the very last moment, according to Smith's later account of the incident, Powhatan's young daughter, Pocahontas, ran forward and placed her head upon his to save him from death.

Perhaps Pocahontas was truly smitten with John Smith—though the bruised and half-starved man in tattered clothing must have presented a sorry sight. Perhaps shrewd old Powhatan had urged his daughter to throw herself upon Smith, knowing full well that his hot-headed braves would not dare to lay a hand on a child of the chief. Powhatan may have feared reprisals from the force of English soldiers that Smith had told him were on the way.

It may seem strange today that a 12-year-old girl could intervene in such serious tribal decisions and have her wishes obeyed. But some Indian women had a strong voice in tribal affairs, especially among the tribes of the Iroquois Indians. Women could own pro-

Above left: Pocohontas in 1616, the year her husband, John Rolfe, took her back to England with him. It was then nine years since she had saved John Smith's life in the Powhatan village.

Above: the illustration that appeared in John Smith's book, showing how the 12-year-old girl Pocohontas had saved his life. Smith lies facing upward, with the two Indians with clubs ready to strike as the chief's daughter comes and kneels beside the condemned man.

perty, speak in councils, and even serve as chiefs. They were often sent on peace missions to other tribes, and in general were accorded greater respect and allowed more personal freedom than the women of Europe during this period.

After Pocahontas had rescued John Smith, Powhatan adopted the Englishman, gave him an Indian name, and sent him back to Jamestown with provisions. In fact, the Indians helped the colonists with gifts of food many times in the ensuing years. But despite their aid, the Virginia settlement almost collapsed during the first few years. Of the 900 colonists who were brought over in successive waves from 1607 to 1609, fewer than 100 remained alive in 1610. In large part, this was because the settlers were not only inexperienced but almost incurably lazy. During his term as president of the colony, from 1608 to 1609, John Smith forced the Jamestown residents to work hard for their survival, imposing harsh punishments on those who did not give their best efforts to the settlement. Smith himself set the pace, toiling every day in the fields, or hacking down trees for firewood and new buildings. Anyone who refused to work hard was left to starve on the other side of the river, and all deserters were shot.

Above: the earliest known picture of a tobacco plant, a woodcut from a book published in Antwerp in 1576. The struggling settlement of Jamestown was given a new lease on life when John Rolfe produced a mild variety of tobacco that would suit Europeans.

Right: tobacco was a familiar part of Indian life, used mainly for ceremonial occasions. This portrait of Chief Tishcohan, one of the chiefs with whom William Penn signed a treaty, shows his tobacco pouch around his neck.

Such brutal discipline seems to have been necessary, for after
Smith returned to England in 1609, having been wounded in a
gunpowder accident, the colony foundered. Doctor Simons, who
remained in Jamestown, wrote that "the savages no sooner realized
that Smith was gone, than they all revolted and murdered any white
man they met. . . . Now we all cried for the loss of Captain Smith,
even his greatest enemies cursed his loss, for we had no more corn
or contributions from the savages, but only mortal wounds from
clubs and arrows. Of the 500 people left behind after Smith's
departure, six months later there remained only 60 men, women, and
children, most miserable and poor creatures, who survived on roots,
herbs, acorns, walnuts, berries, and now and then a little fish. So
great was our famine that a savage we slew and buried was dug up
by some and eaten. . . . This was the time we called the starving
time, which was too vile to describe and scarce to be believed. . . ."

Indeed, the colony was but "10 days from death," when the fleet
of England's Lord De la Warr, the colony's governor, appeared on
the coast, bearing 150 colonists and a store of provisions. Despite
the Jamestown survivors' pleas to be taken back to England with
him, De la Warr forced them to stay on in the colony which, as one
of the new settlers remarked, looked more like the "ruins of some
ancient fortification, than that any people living might now inhabit
it."

HUDSON
BAY

The Great Lakes

GULF OF
ST. LAWRENCE

NEWFOUNDLAND

Nova Scotia

SABLE I.

APPALACHIAN MTS.

New England

PENOBSCOT BAY

Kennebec

Connecticut

Hudson

St. Lawrence

Salem
Boston
MASSACHUSETTS BAY
Plymouth
Providence
RHODE I.
NANTUCKET
MARTHA'S VINEYARD
ELIZABETH IS.
LONG I.

ATLANTIC

OCEAN

DELAWARE B.

CHESAPEAKE
BAY

James Williamsburg
Jamestown
Roanoke
ROANOKE I.
C. Hatteras
PAMLICO SD.

Ohio

Mississippi

Florida

Mississippi
Delta

GULF OF

MEXICO

BAHAMA
ISLANDS

CUBA

HISPANIOLA

TROPIC OF CANCER

	Gilbert	1	1583
	Raleigh's expeditions under:		
	Barlow (with Amades)	2a	1584
	Grenville (with Lane & White)	2b	1585-6
	White	2c	1587
	Gosnold	3	1602
	Waymouth (with Rosier)	4	1605
	Smith (for the London Company)	5a	1606-9
	Smith (for the Plymouth Company)	5b	1614

100   0   100   200   300   400   500
Miles

© Geographical Proje

80°   70°   60°   50°

90°   80°   70°

For the next nine years, the Virginia colony grew slowly under the harsh rule of one of Governor De la Warr's deputies, Thomas Dale. For a time, the settlers continued to suffer the agonies of extreme privation and isolation. In 1612, however, Jamestown's future was saved by a man named John Rolfe, who developed a new cash crop: tobacco. Rolfe probably brought tobacco seed from South America and improved the curing of tobacco leaves until he produced a sweet variety that suited European tastes. A craze for smoking Virginia tobacco soon developed in England, and Jamestown began to show signs of becoming an economic success. The momentous consequences of Rolfe's development were accelerated later on, when the first Negro slaves were sold to the colony by Dutch traders. Using this forced labor, Virginia was soon exporting 500,000 pounds of tobacco every year.

Rolfe celebrated the success of his invention by marrying Pocahontas. The wedding took place in April, 1614, with the full approval of Powhatan, who sent three of his relatives to witness the ceremony. Afterward, diplomatic relations between the Powhatan confederacy and the Virginia colony were resumed. With the return of peace, trade flourished between the Indians and the Jamestown settlers.

In 1616, Rolfe took Pocahontas to England, where she was described as "the Lady Rebecca, alias Pocahontas, who was taught by John Rolfe, her husband, and his friends, to speak English and

Left: the eastern United States, showing the routes of the first Englishmen who explored and began to settle on the Atlantic seaboard between the years 1583 and 1614.

Right: the Jamestown massacre of 1622. Powhatan's brother, Opechancanough, and his warriors attacked all the English plantations simultaneously, killing more than 10 percent of the settlers.

learn English customs and manners. She also had a child by him, and the Treasurer [of the London Company of Virginia] took responsibility for the welfare of both mother and child; besides there were many persons of great rank who were very kind to her." But at the age of 21—just as Rolfe was about to return with her to Virginia—Pocahontas contracted smallpox and died.

Back in Virginia, Pocahontas' fellow tribesmen fared little better. As tobacco became a source of profit, a number of wealthy noblemen and stockholders in the Virginia Company of London were given large grants of land along the James River. Tobacco was the chief crop on all of these "plantations," but it used up the soil and fresh fields were required every few years. Instead of clearing their own land, the plantation owners drove the Indians from their cornfields and took over the land they had cleared. The Indians grew angry and resentful, and war became inevitable. In 1622, under Opechancanough, probably Powhatan's brother, the Indians launched a lightning

Above: the ruins of Jamestown, Virginia, on the James River, as seen by an artist in the 1800's. Originally situated on a fever-infested swamp in the heart of Indian territory, the settlement was eventually abandoned for the better-situated Williamsburg.

attack on all the plantations simultaneously, killing 347 of the 3,000 or so settlers. The English retaliated, and over the next two decades, the combined might of the Powhatan tribes was broken by the Europeans' superior military tactics. The victorious settlers then split up the Powhatan confederacy, and drove the remnants of the various tribes westward.

Meanwhile, the uncompromising rule of Thomas Dale had been replaced, in 1619, by a more democratic form of government, the House of Burgesses. It was the first representative legislative body in America, and continued to play an important part in governing Virginia even after 1624, when King James I made the settlement a royal colony with a governor appointed by himself. Meanwhile, Virginia continued to grow and prosper as more and more colonists flocked to its shores to seek their fortune in the New World. Raleigh's dream of an "Inglishe nation" in America was well on its way to fulfillment.

Above: Wren Building, at the College of William and Mary in Williamsburg, Virginia. The oldest American academic building in use, it was erected at Middle Plantation—where Williamsburg now stands—in 1695 from plans said to have been made by Christopher Wren.

New England's Bays and Rivers 5

While the London Company was busy sending wave after wave of settlers to Jamestown, the Plymouth Company had not been idle. Under the terms of the 1606 agreement that had divided the Virginia Company in two, the Plymouth group was entitled to found a colony in the region between Maine and Maryland. Intending to get a head start on their London associates, the Plymouth merchants had already dispatched one expedition when the first Jamestown settlers left England in December, 1606. But the first Plymouth expedition fell prey to the Spanish in the West Indies. And the second, which set out in May, 1607, did not fare much better. True, the little band did succeed in reaching the coast of Maine, and even established an outpost, called the Popham Plantation, near the mouth of the Kennebec River. But, after one "extreme, unseasonable, and frosty" winter, the Maine settlers gave up and sailed for home.

The New England region, or "northern Virginia," as it was called then, was almost wholly unknown territory in the early 1600's. That the English knew anything at all about it was due to the efforts of two merchant-adventurers, who had explored its coastline shortly before the Plymouth Company was founded.

The first of these merchant-adventurers was Captain Bartholomew Gosnold, who sailed to northern Virginia early in 1602 in search of sassafras. Tea made from the bark of the sassafras tree—which grows throughout the eastern half of North America—was then believed to be a general cure for many types of diseases. A cargo of sassafras was sure to bring a high price in Europe, and Gosnold hoped to make his fortune. He was taking a risk in making the voyage, for he sailed without the permission of Sir Walter Raleigh, who at that time was still governor of all of Virginia. The penalties for infringing on another's royal charter could be stiff, but Gosnold was willing to take a chance in order to earn a quick profit.

On May 14, 1602, after a stormy voyage of nearly two months, Captain Gosnold's ship, the *Concord,* reached the rocky shores of Maine. Great was the surprise of both captain and crew when,

The Pilgrim Fathers leaving Plymouth in 1620. From all reports, the actual departure was a much quieter affair, with the Pilgrims embarking without ceremony and quietly slipping away from the harbor to the open ocean.

Left: Bartholomew Gosnold at Cuttyhunk in "northern Virginia," the area that is now known as New England. He had sailed to the New World in the hope of finding sassafras trees, because the bark was in great demand as a medicine in Europe. His reports of the richness of the soil and the abundant fishing helped kindle English interest in the possibilities of settlement there.

Left: Gosnold was able to win the friendship of the local Indians by presenting them not only with trading trinkets but with steel knives, which were much more valuable to them. This engraving shows sailors landing and offering the gifts to the Indians.

shortly after their arrival, they sighted a small European fishing boat manned by six Indians, whose leader was dressed in a sailor's coat and breeches! From this unusually-garbed Indian, Gosnold learned that French fishermen-traders had recently been in the area to fish for cod. Gosnold himself discovered the rich bounty of New England's coastal waters when, a few days later, having sailed south into a large bay, he and his men did some fishing of their own. "Within five or six hours," wrote one of his seamen later, "we had filled our ship with so many cod fish that we threw many of them overboard again, and I am convinced that in March, April, and May this coast has better fishing than in Newfoundland." Appropriately, the arm of land that forms this bay was later named "Cape Cod."

Gosnold rounded the cape and made landings on the islands of Nantucket and Martha's Vineyard where his crew found "strawberries, red and white, as sweet and much bigger than ours in

England, raspberries, gooseberries, and grapes on every tree so that it was impossible to walk without treading on them." Sailing west to the Elizabeth Islands, they found the soil so fertile that seeds of barley, wheat, and oats sowed at random grew to a height of nine inches within two weeks. They also found an abundance of trees—cedars, beeches, and elms, as well as the special tree whose bark they had come in search of—the sassafras.

Gosnold quickly won over the local Indians with gifts of knives and trinkets. In return for this gesture of goodwill, the Indians obligingly helped the sailors cut the sassafras bark from the trees and load it onto the ship. When the hold was full, Gosnold set sail for England, but not before giving his Indian friends a farewell salute with a blast of trumpets.

Back in England late in 1602, Gosnold made a fine profit from his cargo, much to the annoyance of Sir Walter Raleigh, who ordered a full investigation of this illegal voyage to northern Virginia. But at length, the two men made peace, and Gosnold later became one of the first colonists to sail to Jamestown.

In 1605, a second exploratory voyage to the New England coast was made by one Captain George Waymouth. This voyage was sponsored by two wealthy Englishmen, Sir Ferdinando Gorges and Sir John Popham, who had become greatly interested in the possibilities of founding a colony on the coast of Maine.

Captain Waymouth's ship, the *Archangel,* sailed from London in March, 1605, and followed a west-southwesterly course for five weeks. In early May, while still out of sight of land, the crew sighted

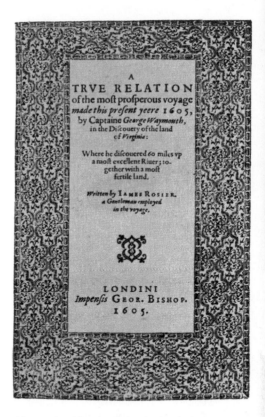

Above: the title page from the book that James Rosier wrote about the voyage to the New England coast with Captain Waymouth on the *Archangel*.

Left: a river in the prosperous, green territory that is now called Maine, along the coast of which Waymouth and Rosier were exploring. The rivers, woods, and virgin meadows stretching off into the unmapped interior seemed to promise inexhaustible riches and a safe place of refuge for dissenters.

a churning rip tide: the *Archangel* had reached Nantucket Sound. Waymouth sailed on to the coast of Cape Cod. Then, rounding the cape, he sailed north to an island off the coast of Maine, where he made a landing. Here he and his men were approached by a group of Indians. According to James Rosier, a seaman on board the *Archangel,* the English sailors greeted them with gifts of "bracelets, rings, and peacock feathers, which they stuck in their hair, [and with] brandy, which they tasted but would not drink, [although] they like sugar candy and raisins." Rosier went on to report that Waymouth's trade with these Indians was very profitable: "For knives, glasses, combs, and other trifles worth four or five shillings, we received 40 good beaver skins."

Captain Waymouth gave the Indians a demonstration of magnetism. "His sword and mine having been touched with the ladestone," writes Rosier, "they attracted a knife and held it fast. . . . The sword made the knife spin on a block, and when we touched it, the knife in turn attracted a needle. This we did to make them believe that we had some great power, so that they would love and fear us." The Indians were then invited aboard the ship, where they "behaved themselves very civilly, neither laughing nor talking all the time, and at supper did not eat like ignorant men, but ate and drank only enough to satisfy them." This restraint seems to have especially impressed the Englishmen, for in Europe at that time it was common for men to make themselves sick by overeating.

Leaving the island, Waymouth explored the Maine coast, and discovered the Kennebec River, of which Rosier wrote: "I would boldly call it the richest, most beautiful, largest, and most secure river and harbour in the world." In so extolling the Kennebec, Rosier was probably thinking of the river's deep and quiet water, which made it much more navigable than the shallow River Thames back in England.

Along the southern coast of Maine, the sailors encountered some hostile Indians who tried to lure them into an ambush. The Englishmen not only avoided the ambush, but succeeded in capturing five of the Indians, whom they took back to England with them. One of the captives was a man named Squanto, who found life in England very much to his liking, and remained in England—by choice—for several years before returning to his native land.

On his return to England, Waymouth gave his employers a glowing report of the Maine region. Popham and Gorges were delighted and, acting on behalf of the Plymouth Company, dispatched a colonizing expedition to the Maine coast in 1607. This was the ill-fated Popham Plantation on the Kennebec River, which had to be abandoned after the first year.

Others besides Gorges and Popham had been interested in Waymouth's report about Maine. English Catholics who were suffering religious persecution at home had begun to seek ways and means of establishing a colony of refuge in the New World. For a time, they considered founding such a colony on the Maine coast. But in the

Above: Squanto, the Indian captured by Waymouth who later became a good friend to the Pilgrims, teaching them a great deal about the wilderness.

Below: "Mrs. Penobscot at the Court of Queen Elizabeth," reputedly the portrait of one of the four Indian women that Sir Ferdinando Gorges brought back from America to the court in the 1500's.

end, it was not Maine, but Maryland that provided an American haven for the persecuted Catholics. In 1632, a Catholic peer named Lord Baltimore was granted a tract of land around Chesapeake Bay, and soon after, established the new colony of Maryland there.

Meanwhile, what of the Plymouth Company's holdings in "northern Virginia"? In 1614, Sir Ferdinando Gorges, annoyed at his fellow merchants' failure to do anything more about exploration or colonization in the New World, contacted Captain John Smith. Smith had returned from Jamestown some five years earlier, and Gorges commissioned him to investigate the shores of northern Virginia. Soon after, Smith sailed west, and explored the coast from Cape Cod to Penobscot Bay. He returned with an enthusiastic report of the Massachusetts coast. "Of all the four uninhabited parts of the world that I have seen," he wrote, "I would rather live and plant a colony here than anywhere else. . . . Plymouth Bay has an excellent harbour, good land, and needs only industrious people."

Delighted, Gorges sent Smith off the following year to plant a colony in this promising land. But his ship never reached America. It was captured by French pirates on the way over. John Smith himself was kept a prisoner by the French for some six months, a period of enforced inactivity that he put to good advantage by making a detailed map of the coast of northern Virginia, which he had renamed "New England." This map was to prove of vital importance to a historic little band of colonists who set out for America some four years later in a vessel called the *Mayflower*.

The Catholics were not the only religious group being persecuted in England at this time. Certain Protestant sects were also under

Above: the capture of John Smith by the French. In the upper left corner he is shown making his landfall on French territory. He was on his way to set up a colony in the land of Massachusetts, about which he had made such an enthusiastic report in 1614.

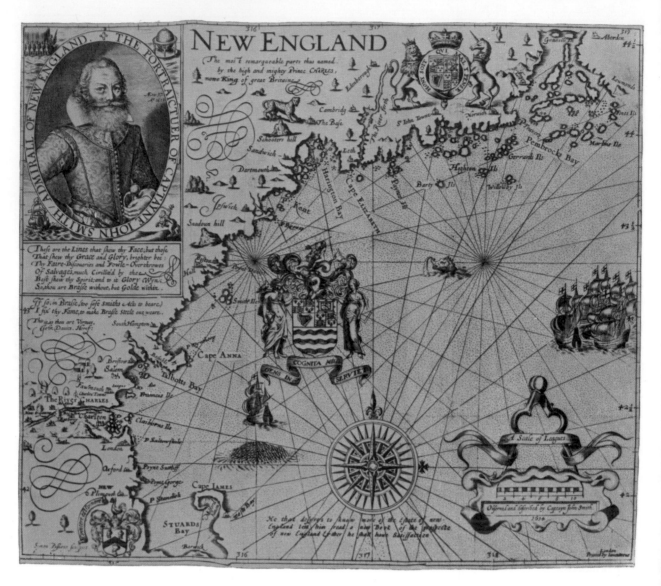

Above: John Smith's map of New England, which the Pilgrims used in 1620 to find their way along the coast and into Plymouth Harbor.
Below: a Delft tile of the early 1600's, with a ship the size of the *Mayflower*.

attack. Although the Church of England had freed itself from papal control and become a strongly Protestant institution, some of the English Calvinists—the "Puritans"—were still dissatisfied with it. They resented the control over the church exercised by the king and his bishops, and wanted a "purer" form of Protestantism—one that upheld a rigorous moral code and relied solely on the teachings of the Bible. Some groups of Puritans were known as "Separatists" because they believed in separating themselves entirely from the Church of England. These views made them very unpopular in England.

In 1608, a group of Separatists, under the leadership of William Brewster, had emigrated to Leiden, in The Netherlands, seeking refuge from the persecution they suffered at home. But, after several years there, they found themselves disenchanted with the life in a foreign country. Deciding that their best hope lay in founding a new community where they could worship as they pleased *and*

Right: the patent of Plymouth Colony. Issued in 1621, it gave the Pilgrims actual title to the lands they had taken. Up until then legally they had been squatters. This patent gave no powers of government, which only the king could grant, and so the only basis of government organization in the colony was still the *Mayflower* compact.

Below: the Pilgrims going to church, walking through the snow carrying their Bibles. The guns were for protection against hostile Indians. Presumably this would be during their first winter, before they had established their friendship with Chief Samoset.

keep their English way of life, they made plans to sail to the New World. They found financial backing from a group of like-minded London merchants and, on September 16, 1620, set out from Plymouth, England in the *Mayflower*. On board were 102 passengers, of whom about 50 were "strangers"—that is, tradesmen, craftsmen, and soldiers (such as Miles Standish) who had been recruited to help in the building of the new colony.

The intended destination of the Pilgrims, as they called themselves, was southern Virginia. But, after 65 storm-tossed days at sea, they found themselves off the coast of New England. Concluding that God's will had brought them to this spot, they decided to found their colony along New England's shores. They had with them a

copy of John Smith's map of the region, and after some searching, found the "Plimouth harbour" he had indicated on the map (now Plymouth, Massachusetts). Here, on December 26, 1620, they went ashore and began building a cluster of rude dwellings, a storehouse, and a place for meetings and worship.

Even before they landed, the Pilgrims had addressed themselves to the problem of how they should govern themselves. They knew that difficulties lay ahead because they possessed no charter. They were, in fact, illegal immigrants in a land that by rights belonged to the Plymouth Company. Moreover, cut off from English law, the group knew that they would need some rules of internal organization. Accordingly, they drew up an agreement called the *Mayflower Compact*, which provided for the enacting of "just and equall" laws "as shall be thought most meete and convenient for ye generall good of ye colonie." The Pilgrim leaders persuaded 41 men on board to sign the compact. By agreeing in advance on a mode of

Above: the first Thanksgiving. Now a traditional holiday in American life, the first Thanksgiving was a simple celebration of the Pilgrims' first corn harvest and an expression of gratitude to the Indians who had taught them how to plant and fertilize their crop.

Right: John Winthrop, 1588–1649, the governor of the Massachusetts Bay colony. He took advantage of an oversight in the community's charter to set up the headquarters in the colony itself, rather than back in England.

self-government, the Pilgrims not only decided how their little society would function, but also gave their enterprise a semblance of legality that might prove useful in any future conflicts with the English authorities.

The Pilgrims' first winter at Plymouth was an agonizing ordeal. The intense cold permeated their primitive houses, and they found themselves desperately short of food. Almost half the colonists died, and of those who were left by spring, few would have survived another winter had it not been for the kindness shown them by Indians of the region.

During the winter of 1620–1621, the Pilgrims had been aware of the presence of Indians, who, they knew, often watched their activities from the nearby woods. No doubt the Indians were simply observing these intruders to see if they intended any harm. But the colonists believed that the Indians' watchfulness was but a portent of a full-scale attack to come. They braced themselves for such an onslaught, but it never came. Instead, one day in March, 1621, a tall Indian strode into the settlement and hailed the colonists with two words: "Welcome Englishmen!" The speaker was Samoset, a chief of the Pemaquid Indians. He had learned English from fishermen along the coast. Samoset informed the Pilgrims that he was sending for two friends, Massasoit, the chief of the Wampanoag Indians who lived around Plymouth and Squanto, the Indian who had been captured by Captain Waymouth and lived in England for several years.

When Massasoit arrived, the Pilgrims concluded a treaty of peace with him—a treaty that lasted until he died 40 years later. Samoset's friend Squanto was given a warm welcome by the settlers, and soon became a regular visitor, often staying as a guest in the home of the colony's governor, William Bradford. In return for this hospitality, Squanto showed the Pilgrims how to plant corn, where to fish, how to fertilize the soil with fish, and how to stalk and trap wild game.

Squanto's teachings proved invaluable to the Pilgrim settlers. The following fall, to celebrate the bountiful harvest he had helped make possible, they held a three-day festival of thanksgiving, to which they invited all their Indian friends. The Indians—who themselves held annual harvest celebrations—came gladly, bringing gifts of meat and corn. Together, Pilgrims and Indians prepared the feast, sang songs, and played games. Out of this happy occasion grew the American tradition of celebrating Thanksgiving Day.

Some years after the Pilgrim colony began to flourish, another Puritan community, the Massachusetts Bay Colony, was planted in New England. This settlement, established at Salem in 1628, was greatly increased in size in 1630, when 1,000 Puritans came to settle there. The new settlers' leader was a lawyer named John Winthrop and, possibly because of his legal knowledge and skills, this second group of Puritans had been able to obtain a royal charter, which gave them the right to settle and govern a colony in the Massachusetts

Bay area. Like other colonial charters, the Massachusetts Bay Company's patent stipulated that the colony be administered by a governor, assisted by a council. But the charter neglected to mention that the company's administrators should be located in England. Seizing on this oversight, the settlement's governor, John Winthrop, transferred the company's headquarters to Massachusetts itself, and initiated a system by which the citizens of the new colony could have an active say in the settlement's political affairs.

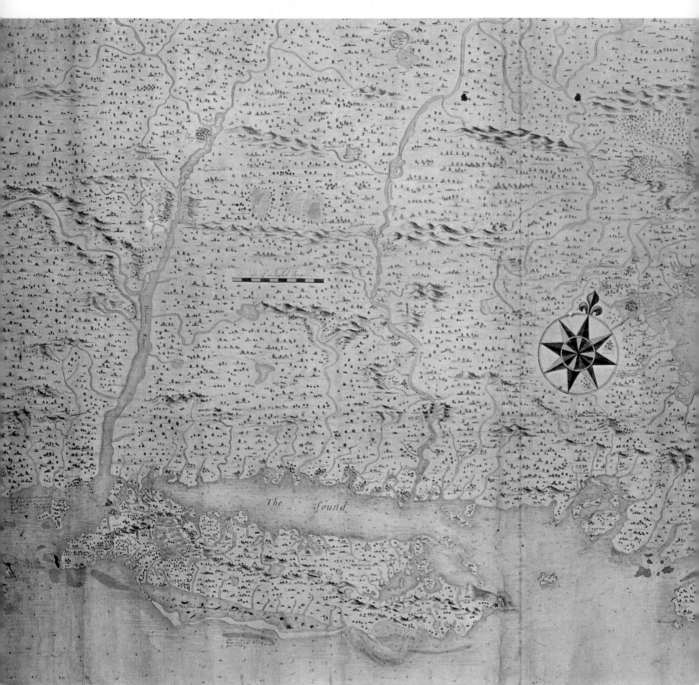

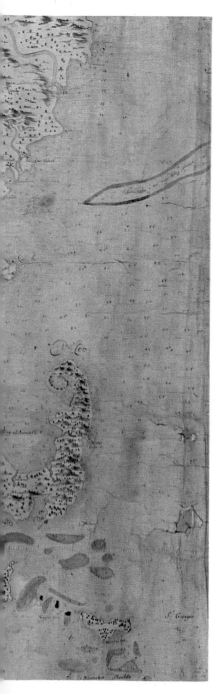

Below: a chart of the coast of New England, drawn in about 1680. As with most new territories, it was the coastal region that was the best known for many years, and the interior that was only gradually mapped accurately as trappers, soldiers, and adventurers probed deeper inland.

Right: one of the early groups to leave the Massachusetts colony, Hooker's party is shown here arriving at the site of Hartford, Connecticut, in 1636.

Right from the beginning, the Massachusetts colony prospered. In 1630, 1,000 picked settlers joined their compatriots there, and by the end of the decade, the Massachusetts Bay Colony had about 10,000 settlers. Towns sprang up quickly throughout the region. By the early 1630's, there were 15 such towns, of which the biggest was Boston, the colony's capital. The Puritans were industrious, and worked hard to establish themselves in the new land as farmers, merchants, craftsmen, fishermen, and shipbuilders.

Politically and economically, the Massachusetts colony was a going concern, but it soon developed religious problems. The Massachusetts Puritans who had sought refuge from religious persecution were themselves persecutors. Dissent from their rigid Puritan beliefs was held to be a crime, and a strict censorship of speech and conduct was set up. One man who dared to raise his voice in protest against this heavy-handed restriction on intellectual freedom was a Separatist named Roger Williams. Among other things, he believed in complete religious freedom for everyone, a conviction which, in 1636, forced him to flee from Massachusetts. Williams and those who shared his beliefs fled to the region of present-day Rhode Island. There they founded a settlement of their own called Providence, where religious freedom was a guaranteed right of every citizen.

Another man who found himself dissatisfied with the strictures of life in Massachusetts was Thomas Hooker, a Congregational preacher who, in 1636, traveled south down the Connecticut River with his family and his congregation, and settled at Hartford in the Connecticut Valley. Still others of Massachusetts' citizens, seeking to increase their land holding, moved north into New Hampshire and Maine.

But the New England expansion was hard on the Indians, who began to find themselves being driven out of their traditional

The figure of the Indians fort or Palizado in
NEW ENGLAND
And the maner of the destroying
It by Captayne Vnderhill
And Captayne Mason

Hear enttera Captayne Vnderhill

The Indians houses

Their Streetes

Hear Enttera Captayne Mason

RH

112

Left: the plan of the fortified Pequot village in Connecticut, showing the 1637 attack by Puritan soldiers and their Indian allies. More than 600 of the inhabitants were massacred.

Right: the Wampanoag chief, King Philip, who led a confederation of tribes against the settlements around Plymouth in 1675. The portrait is on a window shade, and may have been a curtain on a traveling Indian sideshow.

hunting and farming lands. In 1636, a Pequot Indian was accused of murdering a Massachusetts colonist. The colonists' response to this "outrage" was swift and terrible. They burned a Pequot village in Rhode Island. Then in 1637 a force of armed men from the Massachusetts Bay area, together with their Indian allies, marched to a stockaded Pequot village in Connecticut and set it ablaze, coldly shooting down any inhabitants who tried to escape from the inferno. In all, between 600 and 700 Indian men, women, and children died in this brutal massacre. For some 40 years thereafter, the New England colonists were not troubled by the region's Indians. But in 1675, a group of New England tribes, under the leadership of King Philip, the son of Massasoit, attacked settlements in Massachusetts. This started a full-scale war between the colonists and the New England tribes, which lasted about three years. In the end, the settlers routed the Indians, but not before more than 1,000 colonists had been killed and 12 towns destroyed.

During the late 1600's, several of Massachusetts' colonial offshoots received charters of their own, making them colonies on an equal basis with Massachusetts itself: Connecticut in 1662; Rhode Island in 1663 (its second charter—the first was granted to Roger Williams in 1644); and New Hampshire in 1680. Maine, however, remained officially part of Massachusetts until after the Revolutionary War.

And the Plymouth community? This, the first successful Puritan outpost in the New World, the Pilgrims' brave experiment in building a life of their own, never achieved separate status as a royal colony. Instead, it became a ward of the Massachusetts Bay Colony, and lost its distinctive identity entirely in 1691, when it was formally absorbed as part of Massachusetts.

Journael van Herry Hutſon,

Left: title page of Henry Hudson's journal, published in Amsterdam in 1663. Although an Englishman, his voyage in 1609 was for The Netherlands. Below: an imaginative version of Hudson's arrival on Manhattan Island. When they arrived ashore from the *Half Moon* Hudson and his crew were met by the kindly Algonkian Indians who made them very welcome. Originally, Hudson had been sent to find a Northeast Passage to China, but he changed his course in mid-voyage.

When the pioneer farmers of Massachusetts began moving south and west into the Connecticut Valley, they found themselves face to face with a rival group of colonists—the Dutch. For England had not been the only seafaring nation to interest itself in America's Atlantic seaboard during the early 1600's. The Netherlands, too, had established outposts there—outposts that guarded the entire region between the Connecticut Valley and Delaware Bay.

Dutch claims to the mid-Atlantic coastline originated, curiously enough, in a voyage made for The Netherlands by an Englishman, Henry Hudson, in 1609. An expert sailor and navigator, Hudson had already made two voyages for England in search of a northeast passage to Asia around Russia's Arctic seas. Neither attempt had succeeded, but the merchants of The Netherlands, as eager as their English counterparts to discover a new water route to the East, had faith in his navigational skills. In January, 1609, the Dutch East India Company contacted Hudson and hired his services. According to the contract they drew up, the English captain was to "search for a northeast passage, sailing north around Russia until he shall be able to sail south to a latitude of 60°."

On April 6, 1609, Hudson set sail from Amsterdam in a small vessel called the *Half Moon*. Early in the voyage the Dutch and English members of his crew began to quarrel among themselves about how things should be done aboard ship. The English sailors objected to the fact that the cook was a Dutchman, and complained bitterly about the meals he prepared. For their part, the Dutch seamen were annoyed because they were not permitted to eat with the captain as was the custom on Dutch vessels. Hudson finally put an end to these squabbles. But he could not diminish the fears and foreboding that developed among all the members of the crew when the ship entered the northern seas.

Day by day, as the *Half Moon* struggled through increasingly icepacked seas, Hudson's men became more anxious and resentful. When the captain heard them muttering darkly about returning to Amsterdam, he knew that he must do something, and quickly, or he would be faced with a mutiny. Hudson had with him some maps and letters from his friend Captain John Smith that seemed to indicate the presence of a broad, navigable waterway somewhere along the coast of New England. Could this, he had often wondered, be the long-sought Northwest Passage? Hudson showed the docu-

On the map the following labels appear: *PARTE OF*, *The Iland of Manhados*, *PARTE OF THE CONTINENT OF America*, *Hudsons River*, *A Scale of Chaines each conteining four Pearches.*

ments to his restless crew and proposed that they abandon the search for the northeast passage and look for the northwest one instead. He also made it clear that he would have them all hanged as mutineers if they made him return to Amsterdam. Obviously, it was "westward or nothing," and the crew agreed to his plan.

Hudson proceeded across the Atlantic to Newfoundland, and from there sailed south, past Cape Cod, to Chesapeake Bay and on to what is now South Carolina. Although at one point he was only some 60 miles from Jamestown, he did not visit the English colony. He finally turned north again, closely following the shore until he reached the northern coast of present-day New Jersey. There, on September 3, 1609, he reached the large bay that is now called New York Harbor.

No European vessel had been in these waters since 1524, when, it is believed, Giovanni da Verrazano had discovered the bay during his voyage for France. Hudson explored the harbor with extreme caution, constantly taking soundings, and acutely aware that at

Above: a map of Manhattan Island showing part of Long Island, drawn about 1665. The cartographer has carefully drawn in the trees to show how richly forested the island was.

Right: the Indians of the area that is now New York. Both Hudson and the early Dutch settlers on Manhattan Island found the Algonkian Indian tribes living there very helpful.

any moment a strong breeze might blow the ship aground on the sandy bed of the bay. At last, however, he located a deep main channel, and entered the mouth of the great river that now bears his name. Here he sent a party of men ashore to investigate. They soon returned with the happy report that "the land is pleasant, with grass, flowers, and trees that fill the air with sweet smells."

A party of Indians had been seen on shore watching the ship and were invited aboard to trade. One of Hudson's officers later wrote that they were "very polite, [although] we dared not trust them." It was just as well, for a few days later, a group of braves attacked some of the crew, fatally wounding Hudson's mate.

The Indians on Manhattan Island, which Hudson visited on September 12, proved more genuinely friendly. Hudson himself later reported that they were "very good people, for when they saw that I would not remain, they supposed that I was afraid of their bows, and taking their arrows, they broke them into pieces and threw them into the fire." These Indians, an Algonkian tribe, were later to prove immensely helpful to the first Dutch settlers on Manhattan Island.

Hudson took the *Half Moon* some 150 miles up the Hudson River to a point north of present-day Albany. Along the way, he met with various tribes, some of them Iroquois, and did some very profitable trading, exchanging beads, knives, and hatchets for choice beaver and otter skins. But the Indians he encountered near Albany seemed suspicious of the white men. To forestall a possible attack, Hudson invited the local chieftains aboard the ship and, in the words of one of his men, "took them down into the cabin and gave them so much wine that they were all merry." Having thus disarmed the Indians' leaders, Hudson hastily concluded his trading negotiations, and sailed back down the river.

The English captain then made his way back to England, reaching Dartmouth on November 7, 1609. He sent a full report of his voyage to his Dutch employers, and received a request from them that he come to The Netherlands to discuss another journey. But he was prevented from doing so by an order from King James I that forbade all English sailors to hire themselves out to foreign companies.

Thus it was for England, rather than for The Netherlands, that Hudson made his next—and last—voyage in 1610. This time he sailed northwest, past Iceland and Greenland, and discovered

An aerial photograph from 35,000 feet of the ice pack breaking up in Hudson Bay. It was in this icy world that Hudson, his son, and seven of the loyal crew members were set adrift.

Hudson Strait and the immense bay in northeastern Canada now called Hudson Bay. But again the intrepid navigator was troubled by a rebellious crew, and this time neither threats nor promises availed to forestall a mutiny. In the middle of James Bay, a southern extension of Hudson Bay, the crew set Hudson adrift in a small boat with his son John and seven other men. None of the nine was ever seen again.

Meanwhile, the Dutch merchants were already making plans to capitalize on Hudson's explorations for The Netherlands. They had studied his report carefully, and had been quick to see the great fur-trading possibilities of the Hudson Valley. It was not long before many of these merchants were making westward voyages to trade with the Indians in the region that the Dutch now called "New Netherland."

One of these seagoing merchants was Adriaen Block, who journeyed to the mouth of the Hudson in 1614. There, while his

"Hudson's Last Voyage," by John Collier. Hudson appears to have had continual troubles with his crews, but no one will ever know exactly what happened on the ship in Hudson Bay, because the only eye witnesses were the mutinous crew members.

ship lay at anchor, it caught fire and was completely destroyed. Undismayed, Block ordered his crew to construct a new vessel for the voyage home. His sailors did their utmost, but could produce only a makeshift boat some 50 feet long. Afraid that it might not prove strong enough for the journey across the Atlantic, Block decided to stay close to shore for as long as possible. Accordingly, he sailed north through Long Island Sound, hugging the southern coast of Connecticut so that he might find ready shelter for his frail craft in the event of a storm.

Had Block not followed this course, he might have missed the narrow mouth of the waterway that the Pequot Indians called the *Quinnitukut* (meaning "the long, tidal river")—today's Connecticut River. Curious about this *vershe riviere,* or "freshwater river," Block sailed some 45 miles up it to the site of present-day Hartford, and all along the way marveled at the beauty and richness of the surrounding valley. When at last he reached home later in the year, he

GREENLAND

ICELAN

ARCTIC CIRCLE

BAFFIN BAY

LANCASTER SD.

BAFFIN ISLAND

FOXE BASIN

HUDSON STRAIT

RESOLUTION I.

ATLANTIC OCEAN

HUDSON BAY

Labrador

JAMES BAY

NEWFOUNDLAND

GULF OF ST. LAWRENCE

CAPE BRETON I.

The Great Lakes

Nova Scotia

St. Lawrence

Cape Cod

Fort Orange (Albany)

Connecticut

Hudson

Saybrook

NEW NETHERLAND
New Amsterdam
New (New York)
MANHATTAN I.

Wilmington

Ohio

DELAWARE BAY

CHESAPEAKE BAY

Jamestown

– – – Frobisher	**1a,b**	1576, 1577
	1c	1578
——— Hudson	**2a**	1609
Hudson (with Bylot)	**2b**	1610
Hudson (after being set adrift)	**2B**	1610
Mutineers (with Bylot)	**2C**	1610
——— Block	**3**	1614
——— Bylot & Baffin	**4a**	1615
	4b	1616

© Geographical Projects

0 100 200 300 400 500

Left: northeastern Canada and United States, showing attempts made by men such as Hudson and Baffin to find a Northwest Passage to the East in the years between 1576 and 1616.

Right: *Het West Indisch Huys,* West India Company House in Amsterdam, from which the orders went out to govern New Netherland. In all their colonization the main object of the Dutch was to set up and protect profitable trading.

produced a detailed map of the region, and urged the Dutch authorities to assert The Netherlands' claim to it.

In fact, the Dutch were slow to take advantage of Block's explorations in the Connecticut Valley. But they wasted no time in establishing a foothold in the Hudson Valley. As early as 1624, a Dutch fur-trading post called Fort Orange was established on the site of modern Albany. And in 1625, the Dutch West India Company, formed four years earlier, sent a contingent of settlers to found a colony on Manhattan Island.

The Manhattan community, which the Dutch named "New Amsterdam," soon flourished. In its first year, it returned the company's original investment with a highly-profitable cargo of 4,000 beaver pelts and 700 otter skins. In 1626 the Dutch governor of New Netherland, Peter Minuit, purchased the island of Manhattan from the Algonkian. The price he paid—trinkets worth 60 guilders—may have been worth more in the New World at that time than the $24 so often quoted. It was, after all, in the colonists' best interests to deal fairly with this tribe, who had not only brought them gifts of food during the winter, but also kept them supplied with furs for trade. Later, however, when the Dutch began to profit more from their trade with the inland Iroquois, they turned

Below: ships leaving Amsterdam harbor for the Atlantic Ocean, very probably taking emigrants to America. The Dutch West India Company tried to strengthen Dutch claims to their American territory by offering enormous grants of land to settlers who would agree to bring other colonists.

on their Algonkian friends, joining forces with the Iroquois when they made raids on Algonkian villages. The Dutch were first and foremost merchant-traders, and they saw their Indian alliances purely in terms of what was best for business.

To encourage colonization in New Netherland, the Dutch West India Company began offering huge tracts of land to any member of the company who would undertake to bring over at their own expense at least 50 families of settlers within four years. The first of these grants was made in 1629, and others soon followed.

Above: New Amsterdam in 1653, after a watercolor by J. Vinckeboons. At this point the settlement was huddled at the tip of the island, in the area that is now the financial center of the city, with forests covering the rest of the island.

Below: Manhattan today, a photograph by Malcolm Robertson and Alan Brooking showing an Aer Lingus Boeing flying over the city, now an international center of finance, business, and—in the U.N.—world government.

Individual men were given vast estates, rather like feudal manors, in what are now the states of Connecticut, Delaware, New Jersey, and New York. The system was based on the premise that each landowner, or *patroon*, should bring with him tenant farmers to work his land. However, few of the patroons were able to recruit—or to retain—enough farm laborers to work their estates. Nor is it any wonder. Each tenant farmer was required: to pay his landlord a yearly rent of $200; to do three days' service per week for the landlord with his own horse and wagon; to keep up the roads on the estate; and to keep the landlord's storehouse well-stocked with game, wheat, and firewood. Few Dutchmen were willing to subject themselves to this form of economic slavery in the New World, and only one of the patroonships (that of Kiliaen Van Rensselaer on the banks of the Hudson River) ultimately flourished.

New Amsterdam, however, continued to grow and prosper, and soon developed a genuinely cosmopolitan character. Merchants from many lands came to the port to trade, and by 1660 New Amsterdam was supporting a population of more than 1,000. But elsewhere in New Netherland, Dutch power was minimal, and the Dutch found themselves hard put to it to defend their territorial claims against "trespassers" from other nations.

In 1633, word reached the colony's governor, Wouter van Twiller, that Englishmen had been seen in the Connecticut Valley. Van Twiller set out post haste for the region, and built a fort called the "House of Hope" on the present site of Hartford. He also nailed up a proclamation warning the English that they would be severely punished if they tried to settle there. But, in the fall of the very same year, a shipload of Englishmen from the Plymouth Colony blithely sailed up the Connecticut River, ignored the posted warning, and passed directly under the noses of the Dutch gunners— who were so taken aback that they forgot to open fire.

The Plymouth group proceeded to build a settlement about a mile upriver from the fort. Although the two groups were hostile toward each other at first, they soon learned that they would have to cooperate if they were all to survive the winter, and peaceful relations were established. But, after Thomas Hooker and his followers arrived in the valley in 1636, the English settlement became much larger than the Dutch, and the Massachusetts pioneers took to heckling their neighbors in the fort. In 1649, a former governor of New Amsterdam reported that the English "have finally seized the whole of the [Connecticut] River. . . . They have belabored the Company's people with sticks and clubs [and taken] hogs and cows belonging to the fort. . . ." In his report, the ex-governor goes on to enumerate further outrages, and finishes with what must surely have seemed the final insult: "The English have torn down the Dutch coat of arms that had been affixed to a tree, and have carved a ridiculous face in its place!"

The Netherlands complained bitterly that England's colonists had acted "contrary to the laws of nations." But in America,

Below: Peter Stuyvesant (1610–1672) in a portrait on a wooden panel by an unidentified artist. Rigorous in maintaining the position of the Dutch in America, he helped evict the Swedish settlers on the Delaware.

possession was the law, and the Dutch could not hope to keep out the thousands of English settlers who streamed into the Connecticut Valley in the mid-1600's. The Dutch had more success against the Swedish "trespassers" to the south, who, in 1638, had founded a settlement on the Delaware River near the site of present-day Wilmington. In 1655, the Dutch attacked the little colony and ousted the Swedes without much difficulty.

The man who led the attack against New Sweden was New Netherland's governor, Peter Stuyvesant, a tall, stubborn ex-soldier with a booming voice and a wooden leg. Stuyvesant ruled the colony with an iron will, and was almost universally resented. His enemies mockingly called him "Old Silver Nails" for the decorative silver studs he wore on his peg leg. But Stuyvesant did much to promote order and prosperity in New Amsterdam and, if he had had his way, would vastly have increased Dutch power in the New World. The Netherlands, however, refused to grant him the military support he needed to defend Dutch claims in America, despite the obvious fact that New Netherland was rapidly becoming no more than a series of trading posts in English territory.

Nonetheless, the Dutch did control the vital harbor at the mouth of the Hudson. Moreover, their very presence there effectively cut off the English colonies in the north from those in the south. With these thoughts in mind, King Charles II of England took the deliberate step of granting the entire territory between the Connecticut and Delaware rivers to his brother James, Duke of York, in 1664. All that remained was to secure the grant. Accordingly, the Duke sent a fleet of warships to capture New Netherland and, early in September, 1664, after the English show of force, Governor Stuyvesant capitulated. Back in Europe, the Dutch retaliated by

Far left: the early Swedish settlements along the Delaware River, based on a map drawn by Peter Lindstrom in 1654–55. It was these settlements that were attacked by the Dutch in 1655, in an attempt to retain their territory.

Left: Swedish settlers from the Delaware River colony with the Indians. Many land-starved Swedish pioneers left their overcrowded homeland for a fresh start in the New Sweden colony. As with many of the settlements in America success depended largely on good relations with neighboring Indians.

Below: a town plan of Manhattan. Drawn in 1664, it shows The English fleet in the harbor, as Manhattan was taken by the English in that year. Note the street with the wall, which logically became "Wall Street."

declaring war on England—a war that they failed to win. And in 1667, by the Treaty of Breda, New Netherland was officially turned over to England.

Meanwhile, the busy commercial life of New Amsterdam continued unabated. Even after the city had changed hands and been renamed New York, many of the Dutch merchants opted to remain there. It was probably about this time that the name "Yankee" arose, and one theory is that it comes from the common Dutch name Jan Kees—short for Jan Cornelius.

Four new colonies were eventually carved out of New Netherland: New York, New Jersey, Pennsylvania, and Delaware. In 1664, the Duke of York granted the New Jersey region to two aristocratic friends of his, Sir George Carteret and Lord John Berkeley. Ten years later, Berkeley sold his holding to a group of Quakers who wished to escape religious persecution by founding settlements in what became known as "West Jersey." After Carteret's death another group of Quakers bought his section, then known as "East Jersey." In 1702, England united the two colonies as a single royal colony.

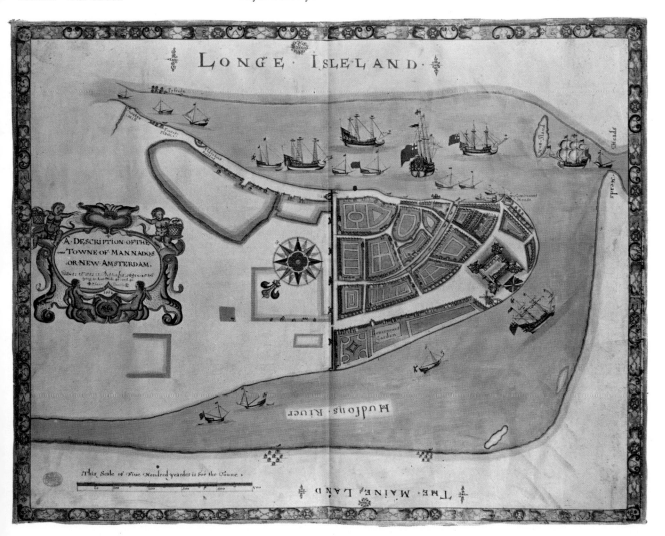

The Dutch Boare Dissected, or a Description of HOGG-LAND.

A *Dutch man* is a Lusty, Fat, two Legged Cheese-Worm: A Creature, that is so addicted to Eating Butter, Drinking fat Drink, and Sliding, that all the World knows him for a slippery Fellow. An *Hollander* is not an *High-lander*, but a *Low-lander*; for he loves to be down in the Dirt, and *Boar*-like, to wallow therein.

THe *Dutch* at first,
  When at the worst,
The *English* did relieve them:
They now for thanks,
  Have play'd base Pranks
With *Englishmen* to grieve them.
A Those Spider-Imps,
  As big as Shrimps,
Doe lively Represent,
  How that the States
  Spin out their Fates
Out of their Bowels vent.
B The *Indian* Ratt
  That runs in at
The Mouth of Crocodile,
  Eates his way through,
  And shews well how
All Nations they beguile.
C The Monstrous Pig,
  With Vipers Big,
That Seven-headed Beast,
  Shews how they still,
  Pay good with ill
To th' *English* and the Rest.
  The Vipers come
  Forth of the Wombe,
With death of their own Mother;
Such are that Nation,
  A Generation,
That rise by fall of Other.
D One of the Rout
  Was Whipt about
Our Streets for telling lyes:
  More of that Nation
  Serv'd in such Fashion
Might be for Forgeries.
E Their Compass is
  An *Holland* Cheese,
To steer a Cup of Ale-by:
  The Knife points forth
  Unto the North
The Needle these Worms sail-by.

F Their Quagmire Isle
  ('Twould make one smile)
In Form lyes like a Custard:
  A Land of Bogs
  To breed up Hogs,
Good Pork with *English* Mustard.
G If any asks,
  What mean the Casks?
'Tis Brandy, that is here:
  And Pickle-Herring,
  (Without all Erring:)
'Tis neither Ale nor Beere.
H Those Two you see,
  That yonder bee
Upon the Bog-Land Walking;
  Are Man and Wife,
  At wofull Strife
About last Night's work talking.
  He Drinks too long,
  Shee gives him Tongue,
In Sharp hot-scolding Pickle,
  With Oyle so glib
  The same for Tib,
Her tipling man to Tickle.
  I Spin all Day,
  You Drink away
More then I get by Wheeling;
  I doe lly part,
  Sayes he, Sweet Heart,
For I doe come home Reeling.
I The *Holland* Boare,
  Hath Stock-Fish store,
As good as can be eaten:
  And such they are,
  As is their Fare,
Scarce good till soundly beaten.
K Their State-House such is,
  It stands on Crutches,
Or Stilts, like some old Creeple:
L Frogs in great Number
  Their Land doth Cumber,
And such-like Croaking People.

Above: *The Dutch Boare Dissected*, an anti-Dutch broadsheet published in 1665, during the period of Anglo-Dutch rivalry. Among other things, it describes the Dutch as "cheese-worms." The tension between the two countries was not limited to America: at this time the two nations were at war.

Meanwhile, in 1681, yet another Quaker, William Penn, had been granted the vast territory stretching west of the Delaware River between southern New York and northern Maryland. The grant was, in fact, in payment for a large debt owed by Charles II to Penn's father. Penn named the heavily-wooded region *Sylvania*—from the Latin word for "woods"—and Charles added the prefix "Penn."

Penn's idea was to establish a well-organized community where religious toleration and a humane legal code would prevail, and he set about his task with remarkable energy and thoroughness. He circulated an advertisement for his proposed colony both in England and Europe, stressing the fact that religious freedom would be guaranteed to all settlers who believed in God. Soon hundreds of German Lutherans and French Huguenots, who were hounded for their beliefs in their own land, were flocking to join the English, German, Dutch, and Welsh Quakers in the new colony. Settlers from the German Rhineland soon became known as the "Pennsylvania Dutch." They were called "Dutch" because the word "Deutsch" (meaning "German") was misinterpreted.

Even before the first settlers had arrived, Penn's surveyor had carefully chosen a site for the main city of Philadelphia, and drawn up plans for its construction. Last but not least, Penn went out of his way to make friends with the region's Indians, ensuring an interval of peace that was to last for about 75 years. Penn's original group of settlers dealt absolutely fairly with these Indians. But later settlers in Pennsylvania were not so scrupulously honest, and used the famous "walking purchase" system to cheat the Indians out of their land. According to this system, an Indian would agree to sell as much land as a white buyer could walk around in a day and a half. But unbeknown to the Indians, the white men all too often cleared a path through the woods in advance, and used trained "walkers" to pace off the course.

From their original settlement at Philadelphia, the Pennsylvania settlers gingerly explored the region to the north and west of them, the fertile Susquehanna River Valley. The first white man to follow this river to its source in central New York was Conrad Weiser, a second-generation Pennsylvanian who had lived among the Iroquois as a boy and spoke their language. In the winter of 1736, Weiser was sent on an urgent peace mission to the Iroquois center at Onondaga, in an effort to stave off an anticipated attack on Quaker settlements in northern Pennsylvania. Weiser almost died during

Above: William Penn, in a portrait by Francis Place. A Quaker, Penn was given a grant to vast territory in payment for a debt the king owed his father. It became a haven for religious dissenters. Below: Penn's treaty with the Indians, by Benjamin West. Penn, determined to make friends of the Indians with his policy of justice and honor, created a peace that lasted 75 years.

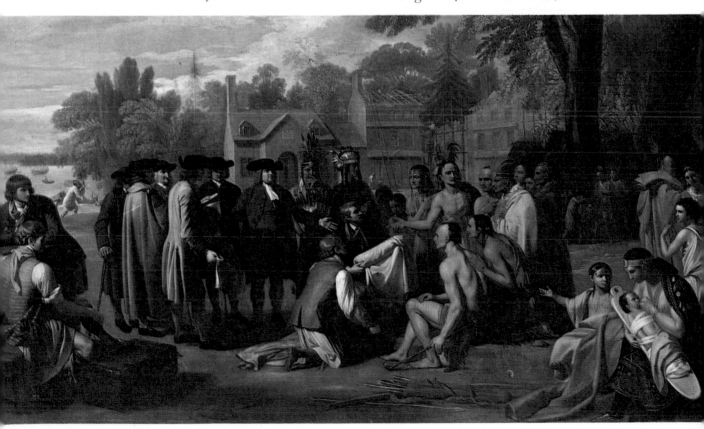

Right: "On the Susquehanna," by Joshua Shaw. The Quakers gradually explored the rich valley through which this river flowed. The peace between the Indians and settlers that existed in Pennsylvania was extended here mainly through the work of Conrad Weiser, a second-generation Pennsylvanian who knew the Iroquois Indians very well.

the journey, the snows were deep, the game scarce, and the forest trails all but invisible. When, despite everything, he reached Onondaga, even the Iroquois were deeply impressed, and agreed to his proposal of peaceful coexistence with the Quaker settlements in the Susquehanna Valley.

The colony of Delaware was originally part of Pennsylvania, but its legislature separated from that of the larger colony in 1701. Nevertheless, it did not become fully independent until 1776, just over a year after the outbreak of the Revolutionary War. By that time, of course, there were 13 English colonies along the Atlantic seaboard. The last three of these were North Carolina and South Carolina, which originated as land grants to a group of titled Englishmen in the late 1600's, and Georgia, which began in 1733 as a haven for England's debtors. The Georgia refuge was the idea of a noted English humanitarian named James Oglethorpe, who had devoted his life to helping the poor and oppressed. But Georgia, like North and South Carolina, soon became a land of opportunity for the rich, rather than for the poor, as wealthy Englishmen began establishing large plantations there and importing African slaves to work the land.

By 1750, there were more than 1 million persons living in the 13 colonies along the Atlantic coast from Maine to Georgia. New towns and homesteads sprang up everywhere, and increasing numbers of colonists began to move inland, driven by an unflinching pioneer spirit that was to become a hallmark of the American character. In doing so, they spread the English sphere of influence far and wide through the eastern wilderness, and gave their French and Spanish rivals in North America increasing cause for alarm.

Right: immigrants on their way to America being welcomed in Leipzig in 1732. They were persecuted Lutherans, who were on their way to Georgia to find a place to live where they would be able to practice their religion.

PREMIER MONASTÈRE DES URSULINES DE QUEBEC
AVEC SES DÉPENDANCES BATI EN 1642, ET BRULÉ EN 1650.

A. DÉPÔT.
B. MONTÉE AU PARLOIR.
C. PETITE SACRISTIE.
D. PORTE EXTÉRIEURE DE LA CHAPELLE DU COUVENT.
E. PARLOIR AU SECOND ÉTAGE PAR LEQUEL LA PLUPART DES RELIGIEUSES ET DES ÉLÈVES, LORS DE L'INCENDIE DU MONASTÈRE EN 1650 S'ÉCHAPPÈRENT EN ROMPANT LES GRILLES.
EF DORTOIR DES RELIGIEUSES.
G.G. INFIRMERIE DES RELIGIEUSES.
H.H. DORTOIR DES ÉLÈVES PENSIONNAIRES.
J. CELLULE QU'OCCUPAIT LA MÈRE MARIE DE L'INCARNATION LORS DE L'INCENDIE.
K. BOULANGER.
L.L. RÉFECTOIRE DES RELIGIEUSES.
M. ANTIQUE FRÊNE, GRANT SÉCULAIRE, SOUS LEQUEL LES RELIGIEUSES, DANS LES PREMIERS TEMPS, INSTRUISAIENT, DANS CHACUNE DE LEURS LANGUES SAUVAGES, ET PRÉPARAIENT AU BAPTÊME, LES NÉOPHYTES, ALGONQUINES, HURONNES, ET MONTAGNAISES.
CE FRÊNE AGÉ AUJOURD'HUI 1847 D'ENVIRONS 500, OFFRE ENCORE AUX SŒURS DU MONASTÈRE SON OMBRE FRAÎCHE, ET DES SOUVENIRS TOUCHANS.
N. MAISON DE MADAME DE LA PELTRIE, BATIE EN 1642 ET DEMOLIE EN 1836.

130

But what of New France during this period of rapid English colonization along the Atlantic seaboard?

In the early 1600's, Champlain's far-flung expeditions had put the French in a position to dominate both the Laurentian Valley and the entire Great Lakes region. But to take full advantage of their expanded sphere of influence, the French needed a strong colonial base on the St. Lawrence. And, after Champlain's death in 1635, New France simply failed to grow.

Unlike the English, the French tended to view the New World chiefly in terms of trade—fish, furs, and a possible westward route to the Indies—rather than as a place to build homes, towns, and a new life. For this reason, few French farmers and tradesmen came to settle in Canada, and by 1660, there were only 3,000 permanent residents there. More than that number of English colonists had settled in Massachusetts in a single year!

Among the brave few who did come to New France during this period were the priests, nuns, and missionaries of the French Catholic Church. Franciscan missionaries had been working in the colony since 1615, and in 1639, nuns of the Ursuline and Hospitalière

Left: the Ursuline Convent in Quebec, built in 1642. It was destroyed by fire in 1650. The Ursuline order has been at the center of life in Quebec since the first nuns arrived there in 1639, to begin their work as both teachers and nurses to the community.

Right: Louis XIV, the Sun King, who was the French monarch during the period after Champlain's death and was determined to keep his American colonies securely under French rule.

orders came to Quebec to teach the children and minister to the sick in the little settlement. In 1642, priests of the Sulpician order established a mission called Ville-Marie on the island of Montreal. Here, with the help of a handful of soldiers, they built and maintained a church and a hospital, despite persistent Iroquois raids.

But perhaps the most dedicated and courageous missionaries in New France were the French Jesuits. Traveling far and wide among the Indians to teach the faith, many of them met barbarous deaths at the hands of the hostile Iroquois. In 1649, for example, a Jesuit

named Father Jean de Brébeuf and his companion, Gabriel Lallemant, were captured and cruelly tortured for many hours with red-hot axes before being put to death.

In fact, Iroquois ambushes, attacks, and massacres were a frequent occurrence throughout the Canadian colony during this time. Nor were these the only hardships borne by the French settlers. Farming was a grim struggle in the stony soil and cold climate of the region, and even the French fur-trading company seemed to be on the

Above: the martyrdom of three of the Jesuits, Fathers Brébeuf and Lallemant at the stakes, and Father Jogues kneeling at the left. This painting by Pommier, a French priest, was made in 1665 from a picture that was part of a map by Bressani drawn in 1657, only eight years after the event.

Left: St. Jean de Brébeuf, one of the Jesuit missionaries who was most cruelly put to death by the Iroquois Indians. He had worked for 13 years in the Huron Indian villages.

Above: Jean Talon, the first *intendant* of New France. He was quick to see the importance of exploration in strengthening the position of the French in their American possessions. Below: Pierre Radisson in a canoe on one of his expeditions into the Great Lakes region. He made the journeys with his brother-in-law, Groseilliers.

brink of ruin. Disease swept through the colony in the early 1660's, and in 1663, the whole area was shaken by an earthquake. But that very year, just as the weary settlers were beginning to cry "Back to France!" King Louis XIV stepped in to save New France. Raising it to the status of a royal province, he equipped it with a regiment of highly-trained soldiers, and appointed a special officer called an *intendant* to head the colonial government and take charge of the colony's internal affairs. The colonial governor was mainly responsible for defense.

The first intendant was a remarkable man named Jean Baptiste Talon. At his urging, the governor instructed the soldiers to build forts all along the St. Lawrence and the southern shores of Lake Ontario to protect New France from the Iroquois. Meanwhile, Talon improved the colony's economic position by establishing local industries like shipbuilding and weaving. Then, to increase the population, he initiated a scheme whereby thousands of young French men and women were recruited to settle in Canada. He encouraged each young couple to have as many children as possible, promising a free grant of 100 acres of land to every father of 12 or more. This plan worked so well that some men eventually petitioned for 200 acres on the grounds of having had a family of 24 or more!

As New France began to revive, Talon turned his attention to exploration. Since Nicolet's voyage in 1634, he learned, only two Frenchmen had dared to venture far into the mysterious lands west of Lake Huron. These two were Médart Chouart, Sieur de Groseilliers, and his brother-in-law, Pierre Ésprit Radisson. Together, the two brothers (as they liked to call themselves) had journeyed farther into the western wilderness than any white men before them. But before they had joined forces, each had had adventures on his own.

In 1652, when Radisson was only 16, he had been captured and "adopted" by the Iroquois Indians in upstate New York. After two years as their prisoner, he had been rescued by some Dutch merchants, who sent him back to France. But once there, he had found European life unbearably tame, and he was soon back in Canada, taking part in a Jesuit expedition deep into Iroquois country.

It was on Radisson's return from this mission that he first met Groseilliers, who himself had just come back from a three-year fur-trading expedition into the interior. In the course of this expedition, Groseilliers had traveled as far as Green Bay on the western shores of Lake Michigan, and had explored the region around Sault Ste. Marie (the falls on the St. Marys River between Lake Huron and Lake Superior). Finding that they shared a love of the wilderness, the two young men began to make plans for a new journey into the interior.

Setting out in 1659, the pair journeyed beyond Sault Ste. Marie, paddling along the southern shores of Lake Superior to Chequamegon Bay. All along the way, they traded with the local Indians, and returned to Montreal in 1660 with a small fortune in furs. The following year, they set off again and this time traveled all the way to the western tip of Lake Superior. From there, they journeyed overland into present-day Minnesota, and became the first white men to meet and trade with the Plains Indians. They then turned north, traveling overland and by canoe as far as north Hudson Bay.

Some years after their return from this extraordinary journey, Radisson and Groseilliers quarreled with the French authorities, and offered their services to King Charles II of England. Under his patronage, they began a series of trading missions to the Hudson Bay region that led, in 1670, to the creation of England's highly-successful Hudson's Bay Company.

Meanwhile, Talon had heard the stories about the young men's wilderness exploits, and determined at once to claim the vast region they had explored for France. Accordingly, in June, 1671, a regal ceremony was performed at Sault Ste. Marie. In the presence of 14 Indian chiefs, a Frenchman called François Daumont, Sieur de St. Lusson, formally asserted France's claim to all the known lands of Canada, together with "all other countries, rivers, lakes, and territories contiguous and adjacent thereunto."

Just about this time, Talon began to hear tantalizing rumors about a great river that flowed south from the Great Lakes region. The priests in the missions that were then being built along the Great Lakes often heard the local Indians speak of this mighty river, though the Indians themselves could not say where it emptied out. A missionary named Father Allouez was one of those who had heard tell of the mysterious river, and it was he who first described it as the "Mississippi," from the Indian words for "great" (missi) and "river" (sipi).

The possibility of such a waterway was of enormous interest to the French authorities. If the river flowed southwest to the Pacific Ocean, it would provide the long-sought passage to Asia. If it

Above: the Mississippi, a vast expanse of water flowing south of the Gulf of Mexico. This view is near La Crosse in Wisconsin, north of the junction with the Wisconsin River where Joliet and his party entered the great river.

Right: Father Jacques Marquette and Louis Joliet meeting with Indians, from a Dutch history of exploration published in the early 1700's. Contacts with the local Indians were important on this kind of expedition, both to help replenish supplies and as a source of information about what lay ahead.

flowed south to the Gulf of Mexico, it would give the French another outlet to the sea for the furs of the Great Lakes region. In either case, French control of the river would serve to check both Spain and England's inland colonial ambitions, and open up the vast American heartland to French exploitation.

With these thoughts in mind, Talon and the new Canadian governor, Louis de Buade, Comte de Frontenac, commissioned an expedition to find and explore the Mississippi. To lead the expedition they chose an adventurous fur trader named Louis Joliet. He was an ideal choice, for he not only knew the Great Lakes area, but possessed the mapmaking skills of a trained cartographer. Joliet was to be accompanied by a party of five men and a Jesuit priest named Father Jacques Marquette. A courageous and dedicated missionary, Marquette had spent several years in the upper lakes area and was fluent in no less than six Indian languages.

Joliet's party set out from the Strait of Mackinac in Lake Michigan in May, 1673, traveling by canoe to Green Bay and thence along the Fox River. A portage of two miles took the men from the lower reaches of the Fox to the Wisconsin River, which they followed west to its junction with the Mississippi. Floating with the current, they proceeded smoothly down the great river, noticing fewer moose and more buffalo along its banks as the northern forests gave way to the open plains of the Midwest. Near the site of present-day St. Louis, their canoes picked up speed, swept along by the turbulent waters of the Missouri, which empties into the Mississippi at this point.

Along the way, the party saw few Indians, and those they did meet were friendly. But when they reached the mouth of the Arkansas River, they found the native peoples hostile and suspicious. Marquette was unfamiliar with the language of these Quapaw tribesmen, but he had the good fortune to find a young Indian who also spoke Illinois, a language he did know. Through this interpreter, he learned of "black gowns" to the south, who "rang bells for prayers." These were almost certainly Spanish priests, which meant that the expedition was nearing the Spanish outposts along the Gulf. Joliet and Marquette took counsel. If they should be captured by the Spaniards or killed by yet more hostile Indians farther south, the fruits of their voyage would be lost. Moreover, they had determined with almost complete certainty that the Mississippi River emptied into the Gulf of Mexico. In fact, they had accomplished their mission, and there was nothing more to do but head for home.

Paddling upriver proved a difficult task, and Father Marquette was taken ill. Anxious to make his report to Talon and Frontenac, Joliet left Marquette in the care of the Green Bay mission, and hurried on alone with his maps and charts. But, while shooting the Lachine rapids above Montreal, Joliet's canoe overturned, and all his precious records of the two-year journey were lost. Fortunately, he was able to make some new maps from memory. And in addition, Marquette still had the journal in which he, too, had recorded many of the expedition's discoveries and observations.

Right: Joliet and Father Marquette being entertained by Indians on their expedition. Until they reached the mouth of the Arkansas River—south of Memphis on what is now the Arkansas/Mississippi state line—all the Indians they encountered were friendly to them.

Above: Louis Henri Buade, Comte de Frontenac, the governor of New France from 1672–82 and 1689–98. He commissioned Joliet to explore the Mississippi and was instrumental in rewarding La Salle for his discoveries.

When Marquette recovered, he returned to the Illinois region to work and teach among the Indians. There, worn out and ailing, he died in 1675, near the shores of Lake Michigan. Joliet took to fur trading once more, ranging through the Canadian forests on expeditions that eventually took him as far north as Hudson Bay.

Perhaps, on one of his visits to the Laurentian colony, Joliet met the man who was destined to take up the thread of Mississippian exploration where he had left off. That man was the intrepid Robert Cavelier, Sieur de La Salle. Born in France of a wealthy family, La Salle had early shown a talent for science and mathematics, and his education had been taken over by the Jesuits. But he had grown up a proud and headstrong young man, with a character ill-suited to the religious discipline. At 21, he had left the priesthood, only to discover that, as a Jesuit, he had been disinherited under French law. Practically penniless, he had set off for the New World to seek his fortune in 1666, at the age of 23.

Soon after he arrived in Canada, La Salle opened a fur-trading post near Montreal. From the Indians he traded with, he learned about the existence of a large river to the southwest called the "Ohio." He became curious about this mysterious waterway, and anxious to

Above: Robert Cavelier, Sieur de La Salle. Born into a wealthy family in France, he spent most of his life in the American wilderness, where at last he realized Talon's vision of extending French power to the Gulf of Mexico.

explore it. Accordingly, in 1669, he sold his trading post and set off for the interior. For the next several years he crisscrossed the region south of the Great Lakes. In the course of his travels, which took him as far south as Illinois, it is reported that he succeeded in locating the Ohio River and in following it south to the rapids above present-day Louisville, Kentucky.

When young La Salle returned to Montreal, Governor Frontenac saw to it that he was amply rewarded for his exploratory efforts. He was honored at the French court and given a tract of land on the site of modern Kingston, Ontario. The location of this land, which included an outpost called Fort Frontenac, soon made La Salle a wealthy man, for all the fur-laden Indian canoes from the interior had to pass by his estate on their way to Montreal. This gave La Salle a chance to bargain for the choicest furs at the lowest cost before the Indian traders reached the buyers farther east.

But the stream of fur-laden canoes passing Fort Frontenac seemed a mere trickle to La Salle. He knew that a vast fortune in beaver pelts lay waiting in the interior. The problem was how to get them to the St. Lawrence faster and in greater bulk. What was needed, he felt, was a European-style vessel that could sail around the Great Lakes from Lake Erie to Lake Superior, trading with the Indians along the way. That such a ship could not travel back from Lake Erie into Lake Ontario, and thence up the St. Lawrence, La Salle already knew. Fear of the Iroquois had thus far prevented French exploration of Niagara Falls, but its existence had been common knowledge since Champlain's time. La Salle's plan was to establish an eastern depot for his ship near the mouth of Lake Erie. Although cargoes would have to be transported from there to the St. Lawrence by canoe, the total time required to get them from the upper lakes to Montreal would still be cut in half.

La Salle set out for Niagara in 1678, accompanied by his best friend Henri de Tonti, by a Franciscan missionary named Father Louis Hennepin, and by a party of workmen. When they reached the Niagara River, La Salle put all hands to work to build a ship and a fort. It was the middle of winter, and he had to urge his men on with threats and occasional rewards of gold pieces.

Above: "The Expedition leaving Fort Frontenac on Lake Ontario, November 18, 1678," by George Catlin. This was the first of Catlin's series on La Salle commissioned by Louis Philippe, king of France in the mid-1800's.

Left: the earliest picture of Niagara Falls, from Father Louis Hennepin's book published in Utrecht in 1697. The French had known about Niagara Falls earlier, but their bad relations with the Iroquois Indians had kept them from actually reaching the falls.

Below: "Portage around the Falls of Niagara, January 22, 1679," the third in the series of 26 paintings by George Catlin on the explorations of La Salle.

The party had brought with them a large quantity of supplies, but even so, La Salle was forced to return to Fort Frontenac for additional materials. There he found himself confronted by his creditors, who angrily demanded payment of the many debts he had already incurred in outfitting his expedition. Putting them off with the promise to pay up as soon as his ship returned from the Great Lakes, La Salle set off once more for Niagara.

During his absence, work on the boat had continued under the watchful eyes of a few hostile Iroquois. While the bulk of the tribe had gone south to fight the Erie Indians, a few of these Iroquois warriors had stayed behind to keep an eye on the strange doings of the white men. The Iroquois continually prowled around the vicinity of the boat, and one day even attacked the smith, who was forced to defend himself with a red-hot iron. This hostile atmosphere had one beneficial result, however, for as Father Hennepin wrote later, it "encouraged our workmen to go on with their work more briskly!" In fact, by the time La Salle returned, in August, 1679, the ship was all but finished, needing only the heavy anchors that he brought with him from Fort Frontenac.

With its heavily-caulked flat bottom and its makeshift deerskin sails, the 60-ton vessel was hardly the pride of the French fleet. Nevertheless, this "winged canoe," as the Indians called it, was about to become the first sailing ship on the Great Lakes. La Salle named it the *Griffin,* in honor of the Comte de Frontenac, whose coat of arms bore two griffins. And, as soon as the last supplies were on board, he weighed anchor and set sail, undeterred by the grumblings of the ship's pilot, who swore that La Salle had brought him into the wilderness "to die in fresh water."

Covering as many as 100 miles a day when the wind was right, the *Griffin* sailed into Lake Erie, Lake Huron, and then into Lake Michigan. Frequent stops were made along the way to trade with the Indians, and soon the ship's hold was bulging with a rich cargo of beaver pelts. La Salle, delighted with the success of his project thus far, began to envisage a whole fleet of ships to ply the inland waterways. Nor did his ambition stop there. He wanted to travel down the length of the Mississippi. He proposed to establish a direct shipping link to the sea and, at the same time, carry out Talon's dream of extending authority as far south as the Gulf of Mexico.

With these thoughts in mind, La Salle ordered some of his men to sail the fur-laden *Griffin* back to Lake Erie, while he, Tonti, and a few of the others made preparations for the journey down the Mississippi. As the *Griffin* sailed away, La Salle and his party left the southeastern shores of Lake Michigan, paddled up the St. Joseph River, and followed the Kankakee River to the Illinois River. Near the site of present-day Peoria, they landed, built a stockade called Fort Crèvecoeur (Fort Heartbreak), and began work on the boat that would take them down to the Gulf.

La Salle had given the *Griffin's* crew orders to return to Lake

Above: "Launching of the *Griffin*," by George Catlin in his La Salle series. Although most of the Iroquois Indians had gone south for a war with the Erie Indians, there were a few who remained as a menacing presence, and the expedition was relieved to get the ship finished and safely underway.

Right: the building of the *Griffin*. It is unlikely that La Salle's workmen had ever built a ship before, much less one furnished with deerskin sails. La Salle's idea was to bring furs from the upper lakes in his ship to the mouth of Lake Erie, thus cutting in half the time that had been required previously to bring furs to Montreal.

Michigan with supplies for the Mississippi venture as soon as they had seen the cargo safely on its way north from Niagara. But three months passed with no word of the *Griffin's* return. La Salle decided to go to Niagara to find out what had happened. Leaving Tonti in charge of Fort Crèvecoeur, he set out in March, 1680, with six Frenchmen and an Indian guide.

The spring thaws were just beginning, and jagged ice floes in the streams and rivers made it impossible to travel by canoe. Patches of slush covered the soggy ground, and even the men's snowshoes became useless. Sinking ankle deep with every step they took through the marshy woodlands, La Salle and his men struggled on until they reached the southeastern shores of Lake Michigan. Here, at the mouth of the St. Joseph River, the *Griffin* was to have made its first stop. But the Indians of the region had seen nothing of the ship. More and more anxious, La Salle hurried on, trudging mile after weary mile until he finally reached Niagara. But alas, there was no sign of the *Griffin* here, either. With a heavy heart, La Salle left his exhausted companions at Niagara, and marched north through the spring rains to Montreal. Here his 1,000 mile journey ended with a confirmation of his worst fears: word had reached Montreal that the ship had gone down in Lake Michigan.

The loss of his fur fortune meant that La Salle once more had no money. But he was persuasive and ambitious, and he managed to borrow enough cash to stave off his creditors and purchase fresh supplies for his Mississippi venture. However, before he could complete his preparations, two coureurs de bois reached him with news of a further disaster. Tonti's men had mutinied. La Salle's absence, the imminent threat of an Iroquois attack, and word of the *Griffin's* fate—which meant that the men would not receive the two years' back pay owed to them—had made them turn on La Salle's lieutenant. Tonti and a few loyal men had been driven into the woods, while the mutineers had destroyed the fort, taken as many supplies as they could carry, and thrown the rest into the river.

Above: "The Chevalier De Tonty Suing For Peace in the Village of the Iroquois," by George Catlin. Tonti was stabbed by one of the warriors as he tried to persuade the Iroquois to let them go. Eventually the wounded man and his companions were released, and managed to make their way north into friendly Ottawa territory.

Above: Henri de Tonti, 1650 ?–1704. He was nicknamed "Iron Hand" on account of the artificial metal hand he wore. He and La Salle became friends in France in 1678 and came to Canada together. The two of them managed to extend greatly the territory of New France through their explorations. Courtesy Chicago Historical Society.

Below: "The Expedition Arriving at the Mouth of the Mississippi; La Salle Erects a Cross and Takes Possession of the Country 'In the Name of Louis Le Grand, King of France and Navarre,' April 9th, 1682," by George Catlin.

La Salle set off immediately to find his friend. By August, 1680, he was back in Illinois country. There, in a recently-abandoned Illinois village, he found a scene of devastation. An Iroquois war party, frustrated and vengeful at finding their intended victims gone, had dug up and mutilated all the bodies in the Illinois' cemeteries. But La Salle found no trace of a white man, which gave him hope that Tonti might still be alive. He hurried 50 miles down the Illinois River to Fort Crèvecoeur. There, amidst the ruins, was the half-finished hull of the boat. On the side of the vessel, one of Tonti's mutinous crew had scrawled the bleak words, "We are all savages."

La Salle scoured the surrounding territory for some sign of his friend, traveling down the Illinois River to the point at which it joins the Mississippi. Once on the mighty river, he must have been sorely tempted to begin his long-awaited journey to the Gulf of Mexico. But this was not the moment for such a venture. He had with him only four men and meager supplies—and, even more important, he had yet to find Tonti. Sadly, La Salle turned away from the Mississippi and paddled 273 miles back up the Illinois. Then, hoping daily for some word of Tonti, he set out overland for southern Michigan.

But it was to be many months before La Salle learned—through an accidental meeting with some Indians from Wisconsin—that his friend was safe and well. Tonti and his men, they told him, had been captured by the Iroquois, who, for a time, had threatened to murder them. But in the end, Tonti had convinced the Iroquois to let them go, and, half starved and feverish, he and his men had made their way north to Wisconsin. There, they had been taken in and nursed back to health by a friendly Ottawa tribe.

Below: a map of the early 1700's showing the Mississippi region. The expanse of the French possessions at that time is impressive. Through the exploration of Joliet and La Salle, the course of the Mississippi River is quite accurately charted, complete with its main tributaries. The Great Lakes are also reasonably well defined. Compare them with the obviously stunted shape of the Florida peninsula and the uncertainty about the position of the mountains in the "Pays des Apaches"—the land of the Apache. .

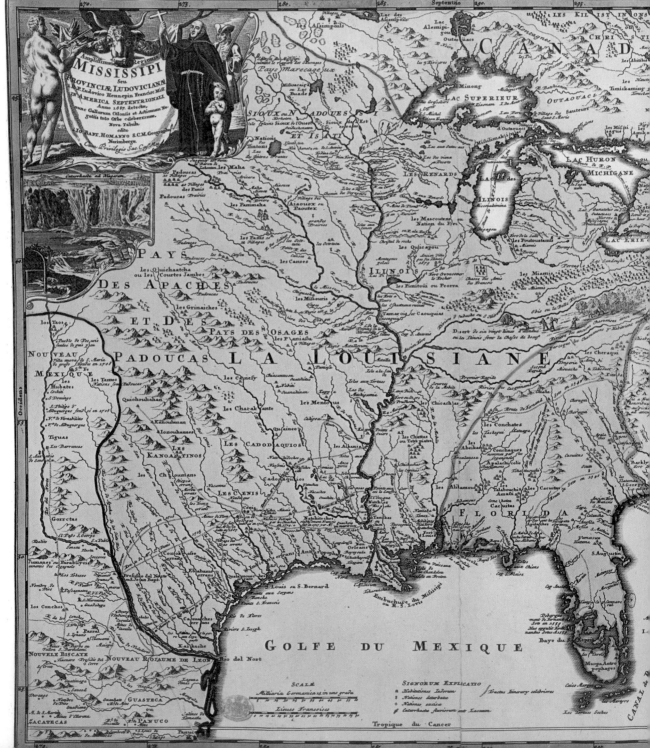

Reunited once more, La Salle and Tonti made preparations for the long-delayed Mississippi expedition. La Salle traveled through the Illinois and Ohio region, recruiting Indians to take part in the venture. At last, with a party of 23 Frenchmen and 18 Indian men and their families, La Salle set out from Fort Miami in December, 1681. It was the dead of winter but, as usual, La Salle was too impatient to wait for better weather. The canoes and supplies were placed on sledges and dragged along the frozen surface of the Illinois River to the Mississippi. Then, in mid-February, 1682, the party began its voyage down the mighty river. Like Joliet and Marquette nine years before, La Salle met only friendly Indians as he proceeded south. But unlike his predecessors, he did not stop when he reached the Arkansas River, but continued south to the Mississippi delta. There, as his men paddled on between the low marshes, La Salle found the water growing gradually saltier. And suddenly, on April 8, 1682, the broad horizon of the Gulf itself appeared before him.

La Salle landed, planted a large wooden cross, and fired off a volley of musket shots. Then, in the name of Louis XIV, he formally took possession of the entire Mississippi Valley for France. But the small party of men he had with him was not enough to establish a permanent post at the mouth of the Mississippi. La Salle decided to go to France to seek royal backing for a large expeditionary force.

La Salle made only one major stop on his way back to the Great Lakes. That was at a point along the Illinois River, where he built a trading post he called Fort St. Louis. Then he returned to the Laurentian Valley and sailed for France. At the French court, his action in claiming the Louisiana territory excited enormous interest. And his heady vision of French supremacy in the American heartland soon won him the king's support for a major expedition to build a port on the Gulf coast.

In August, 1684, La Salle sailed from France with "4 vessels, which had on board 280 persons, including the crews, 100 soldiers with their officers, about 30 gentlemen volunteers, some young women, and the rest hired people and workmen of all sorts necessary for founding a settlement." These are the words of Henri Joutel, a young man who signed on as La Salle's personal aide, and who kept a detailed journal of the voyage—a journal that was to record an almost unending series of disasters.

Quarrels between La Salle and the admiral of the fleet, Beaujeu, began early in the voyage, and soon the two men were completely at odds. When they reached the Caribbean, Spanish pirates captured one of the vessels, and La Salle was taken dangerously ill with some unknown fever. He had recovered by the time the fleet reached the Gulf, but here, a new series of mishaps occurred. The expedition's supply ship ran aground and was destroyed in a storm. Far more serious, the expedition was unable to locate the mouth of the Mississippi. Several shore parties—one of which was led by La Salle himself—went inland to find the main channel of the river. But each time they were misled by the maze of streams, foggy swamps, and

Above: Father Louis Hennepin, 1640–1701, in an anonymous oil portrait painted in 1694. Father Hennepin was a Franciscan missionary in New France.

Above: the murder of La Salle, from Father Hennepin's book. La Salle had sent several discontented men on a routine duty. When they didn't return, he sent his nephew after them. They killed the nephew, and when La Salle came to investigate, he was shot through the head so that, according to Joutel, "he dropped down dead on the spot, without speaking one word."

shallow bays that so effectively hide it. Both officers and crew began to doubt the very existence of the river, and La Salle's honor and credibility were called in question. At last, Beaujeu decided to sail for home, and many of the men opted to go with him. But La Salle refused to give up. He knew his river was close by, and he insisted on remaining behind with a few others to hunt for it.

But the place where La Salle and his party were eventually put ashore was hundreds of miles west of the Mississippi delta—on the Texas coast. Here, at Matagorda Bay, unaware of their true position, La Salle and his followers built a small fort and began a series of fruitless attempts to locate the banks of the Mississippi. At last, in January, 1687, La Salle set off to make one final, desperate search for the great river. With him he took 17 men, including his faithful scribe Joutel. He left behind 20 men to hold the fort at Matagorda.

La Salle's party marched a distance of some 200 miles through bush and swamplands, under the watchful eye of hostile Indians.

After several weeks of this torturous progress, the men began to despair of ever finding the Mississippi. Desperate and frightened, several of them turned on La Salle and, early one morning, shot their commander through the head. Thus, still seeking his river, Robert Cavelier, Sieur de La Salle, died in the wilderness.

For a while, Joutel's life, too, hung in the balance. But he succeeded in getting back to Matagorda and, the following May, set off from there with six other men in an attempt to reach Canada. With the help of an Indian guide, they managed to reach a small French outpost on the Mississippi that had been set up, long before, by the faithful Tonti to greet La Salle and help him on his way up the river. Upon hearing Joutel's story, Tonti made a heroic effort to save the stranded people at Matagorda Bay, but was prevented from reaching them by hostile Indians south of Arkansas. Meanwhile, La Salle's murderers—who knew that they could never return to any area under French control when the truth about them was known—

Above: Father Hennepin captured by the Iroquois Indians, in a plate from his book. His captors, however, were sufficiently impressed by the "magic" of his compass and his silver chalice so that they did not dare to kill him.

147

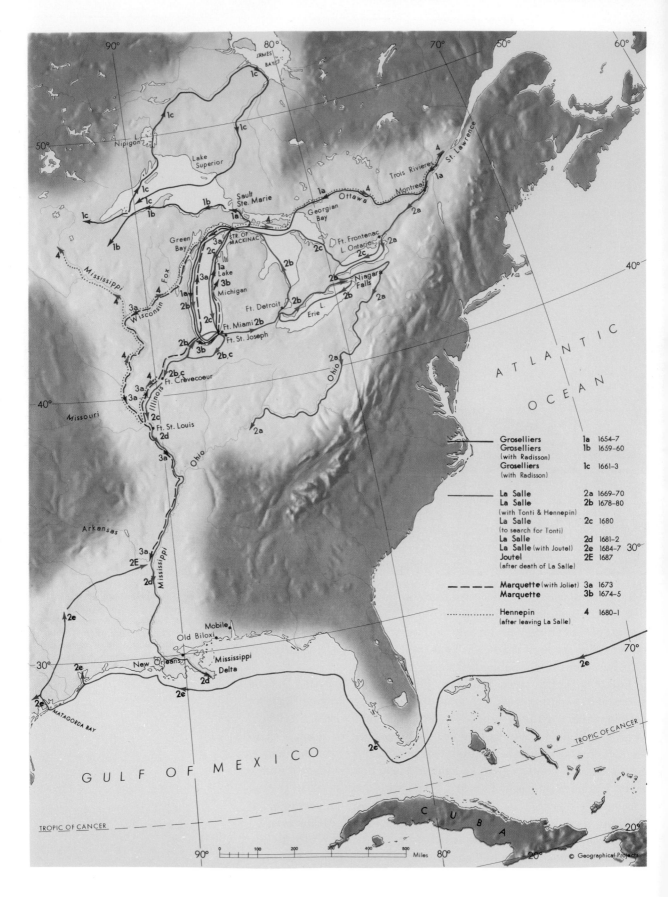

JAMES BAY

L. Nipigon

Lake Superior

Sault Ste. Marie

Green Bay

STR. OF MACKINAC

Lake Michigan

Ft. Detroit

Ft. Miami

Ft. St. Joseph

Erie L.

Ft. Frontenac

L. Ontario

Georgian Bay

Niagara Falls

Ottawa

Montreal

Trois Rivieres

St. Lawrence

Fox

Wisconsin

Mississippi

Ft. Crevecoeur

Illinois

Ft. St. Louis

Missouri

Ohio

Ohio

ATLANTIC OCEAN

Arkansas

Mississippi

Mobile

Old Biloxi

New Orleans

Mississippi Delta

MATAGORDA BAY

TROPIC OF CANCER

GULF OF MEXICO

CUBA

TROPIC OF CANCER

Groselliers   1a   1654–7
Groselliers   1b   1659–60
(with Radisson)
Groselliers   1c   1661–3
(with Radisson)

La Salle   2a   1669–70
La Salle   2b   1678–80
(with Tonti & Hennepin)
La Salle   2c   1680
(to search for Tonti)
La Salle   2d   1681–2
La Salle (with Joutel)   2e   1684–7
Joutel   2E   1687
(after death of La Salle)

Marquette (with Joliet)   3a   1673
Marquette   3b   1674–5

Hennepin   4   1680–1
(after leaving La Salle)

Miles

© Geographical Projects

Left: the central and eastern United States, showing the routes of French explorers such as Groselliers and La Salle up and down the Mississippi River between 1654 and 1687.

were captured by a hostile tribe, who first enslaved them, and then turned them over to the Spanish. The Matagorda settlement vanished without a trace.

The failure of La Salle's expedition, however, did not put an end to French attempts to expand their sphere of influence in North America. Even before La Salle's death, Tonti's cousin, Daniel Greysolon, Sieur Duluth, had explored the upper reaches of the Mississippi and claimed much of the country beyond it for France. A curious sidelight of Duluth's expedition was his rescue of Father Hennepin who, in 1679, had set off to explore the southern Illinois River and been captured by the Sioux. The Indians had starved and taunted him, but had spared his life because they believed he could summon supernatural forces with his magnetic compass and his silver chalice. Duluth's fortuitous arrival with a party of armed men in 1680 released the missionary from his miserable captivity.

In the 1690's, the French increased the number of their outposts in the Great Lakes region and began building forts southward along the Mississippi. The northern anchor of this system of fortifications was Fort Pontchartrain, commonly called Fort Detroit, a post established by Antoine de la Mothe Cadillac in the Michigan region west of Lake Erie. In 1699, a French-Canadian explorer named Pierre le Moyne, Sieur d'Iberville, established an outpost at Old Biloxi (now Ocean Springs), on the Gulf Coast, and three years later, another French fort was built at Mobile. Finally, in 1718, La Salle's cherished dream of a port at the mouth of the Mississippi was realized with the building of New Orleans, capital of Louisiana and southernmost citadel of the French in North America.

But for how long could the French maintain their grasp over these vast regions of the American continent? Already there had been clashes with the Spanish to the south and with the English to the northeast. Sooner or later, there was bound to be a monumental collision as the various territorial claims made by the three nations—and particularly those made by France and England—began to overlap and conflict.

Below: New Orleans in 1726, only eight years after its founding, in the earliest known picture of the city.

Fighting for the Land

8

Above: "The Death of Wolfe," a painting by Benjamin West (1738–1820). The battle for Quebec cost the lives of both the British and French generals. It was only one of the battles over possession of the American continent.

Left: James Wolfe. His conquest of Louisbourg not only safeguarded New England, but opened the way to Quebec. When Quebec fell in September, 1759, Canada had been won for the British.

In the late 1600's, as the exploration and colonization of North America gathered momentum, an important question began to be asked in the courts of Europe: Which of the great powers would ultimately control the vast American continent? Spain, France, and England had all made territorial claims there, and those claims had begun to conflict dangerously. In the 1690's, there were clashes between the French and the Spanish on the Gulf Coast, and between the Spanish and the English south of the Carolinas. But the most serious conflict of interests was between the English and the French, whose rival claims in New York, New England, and the Hudson Bay

151

area provoked many a bloody skirmish during the late 1600's. These skirmishes were part of a desultory and inconclusive struggle called "King William's War," which dragged on from 1689 to 1697.

Anglo-French territorial conflicts came to a head in a series of major wars during the 1700's. Ostensibly, the wars originated in purely European issues. But each Anglo-French war in Europe was used as an excuse to pursue the territorial struggle in America. And significantly, all of the treaties which ended the wars included provisions stating exactly who had won what in the American provinces. Of course, the French and British frontiersmen in those provinces paid little attention to the treaties. It took a long time for European news to reach America, and even when it did, orders from abroad were not likely to stop the farmers and fur traders from fighting for their land.

The first of the wars in the 1700's was the War of Spanish Succession (1702–1713). In America, where it was called "Queen Anne's War," the struggle took place in New England and in the Florida and South Carolina regions. Both in the north and in the south, the French—aided by the Spanish—fought hard, but were defeated. Great Britain emerged triumphant from the conflict, having added the Hudson Bay region, Newfoundland, and Acadia (as the French then called Nova Scotia) to the American regions under her control.

To counter these losses, the French stepped up their fort-building activities east of the Mississippi, with the idea of keeping the English boxed in behind the Appalachians. But the French could not hope to contain their British rivals, they simply did not have the strength. To begin with, by 1760 the entire population of New France was only about 60,000, while the population of the 13 British colonies numbered over 1,500,000. Moreover, unlike their British counterparts, the French settlers had developed no home industries, and were heavily dependent on an unreliable supply of provisions and equipment from abroad. New France prided itself on its permanent force of professional soldiers. But the average French-Canadian lacked the fierce spirit of independence and self-reliance that made even the improvised citizen militias of the British colonies formidable opponents. Last but not least, the French had never succeeded in winning over the hostile Iroquois, who, as early as the mid-1600's, had begun siding with the British in their quarrels with the French.

A new European conflict, the War of the Austrian Succession, broke out in 1744. In America, where it was called "King George's War," the struggle led to the British capture of Fort Louisbourg on Cape Breton Island. The sudden conquest of this major port, surprised the British as much as it did the French. Nevertheless, the British deeply resented the provision in the Treaty of Aix-la-Chapelle that forced them to relinquish their prize in 1748.

Perhaps this was why, the following year, the British king gave his blessing to a scheme that was certain to anger the French. The crown granted 200,000 acres of land in the upper Ohio Valley to a

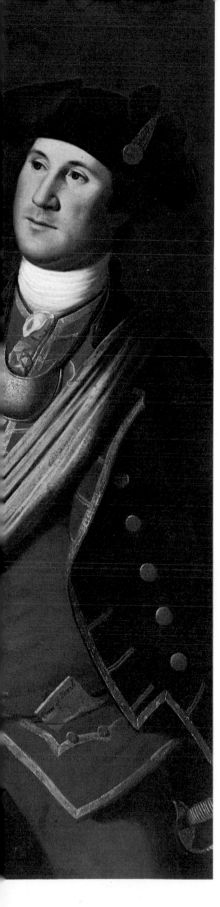

Left: a portrait of Colonel Washington of the Virginia militia, by C. W. Peale. Even early in his military career he had a fine tactical sense and could adjust his strategy to unorthodox situations.

Below: Newfoundland in 1692, a chart of the coastlines, with the fishing districts marked. Note how the fishing grounds have fleets marked English, French, and Maine (American). Not only was the land jealously claimed but the sea, also, was under dispute.

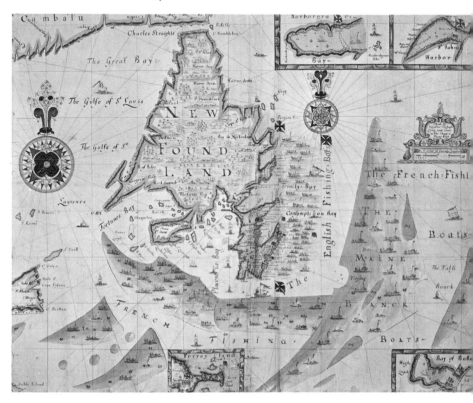

group of Virginians and London merchants who wished to trade and settle there. This was the very region to which French fur traders were already staking their claims. Not surprisingly, the French resented the Virginian interlopers, and sent an armed force to oust them. Moreover, the French began building a chain of forts from Lake Erie to the Ohio River to secure their own claim to the area. One of these forts, built in 1754 on the site of present-day Pittsburgh, was Fort Duquesne. The very next year, Virginia sent a group of volunteer soldiers under General Braddock to attack the French stronghold. One of the officers was a young Virginian named George Washington. He strongly urged Braddock to use the Indians' own guerrilla tactics against the French and their Indian allies. But Braddock insisted on relying on traditional European fighting methods. The result was a disaster, in which the general and many of his men were killed. Only young Washington's courage and cool-headedness saved the rest.

The battle at Fort Duquesne took place, in fact, between wars. The next major European conflict, the Seven Years' War, did not begin until 1756. Nevertheless, the Americans saw this third war as a continuation of the Ohio Valley struggle, and simply called it the French and Indian War.

The effect of this Anglo-French confrontation on the balance of power in North America proved decisive. In 1758, the British retook Louisbourg, the key to the St. Lawrence River and to the safety of New England. The news of the event was celebrated with giant bonfires in London, Philadelphia, Boston, and New York. In the same year, Fort Duquesne was captured by a British force—again one that included George Washington, much to his satisfaction. But the most important British victory in America was the capture of Quebec in 1759. Under the leadership of General James Wolfe, a large British force sailed down the St. Lawrence to Quebec. After a

Below: North America in 1700. By this time three European powers—France, Spain, and England—were firmly established in the south and east of the continent. But it was between France and England that the great conflict for supremacy took place in a series of major wars in the 1700's.

British possessions 1700

French possessions 1700

Spanish possessions 1700

Areas claimed by British & French

© Geographical Projects

siege of almost three months, Wolfe's army stormed the Heights of Abraham above the city. Quebec, guarded by a smaller force of French soldiers under Marquis de Montcalm, was at last forced to surrender, but not before both generals had been fatally wounded. Wolfe lived just long enough to know that he had won Canada for Britain. British supremacy there was further assured the following year when Montreal was captured.

By the Treaty of Paris in 1763, France formally turned over to Britain not only Canada but also all her possessions east of the Mississippi River, with the exception of New Orleans, which France ceded to Spain in return for the help Spain had given the French during the war. Spain also received all French land west of the Mississippi. But, on her side, Spain was forced to turn over all her Florida holdings to Britain.

The year 1763 marked a momentous turning point in American

Below: North America in 1763. After a series of victories over the combined armies of France and Spain in both America and Europe, Britain now reigned supreme over the whole eastern half of the continent. It was not until 1776, when the Thirteen Colonies rebelled, that Britain's supremacy was challenged.

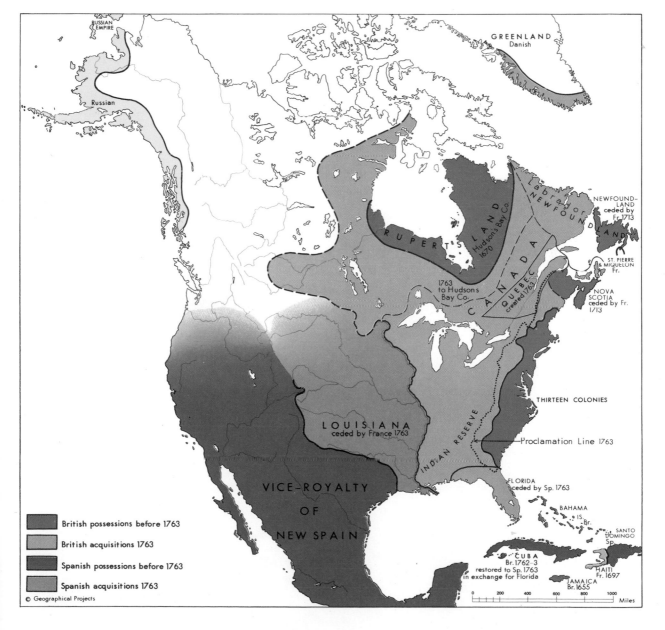

history. Britain now reigned supreme over the whole eastern half of the continent, and her right to do so was not again challenged until 1776, when the Thirteen Colonies themselves rebelled against British rule.

Meanwhile, British colonial expansion continued at breakneck speed, both along the Atlantic coast and westward, toward the foothills of the Appalachians. Everywhere in the fast-growing colonies—from New Hampshire to Georgia—there were land-hungry men eager and willing to seek their fortunes in the virgin wilderness beyond the existing frontiers. Moreover, after 1763, the British colonists who wanted to travel beyond the Appalachians might do so without fear of reprisals from the French. Even so, the men and women who set out to tame the primeval forests of the interior had to be both strong and courageous, for the life of the pioneer was one of unremitting hardship, backbreaking labor, and the constant threat of Indian attack.

One man who proved himself eminently successful in dealing with all the problems and perils of the wilderness was Daniel Boone. Born in a log cabin in Pennsylvania in 1734, Boone spent his boyhood years learning the ways of the woods: how to stalk every kind of game; how to survive in the open in all weathers; and, perhaps most important, how to outfox a hostile Indian. When young Daniel was 16, his family moved to the wild frontier country in North Carolina, where it was his job to keep the family larder well stocked with game. In 1755, Boone took part in the struggle to wrest Fort Duquesne from the French, and it was on this campaign that he first heard tales of the beautiful Kentucky wilderness beyond the Appalachian highlands. Then and there, Boone became determined to see this wonderful region, but almost 14 years elapsed before he was finally able to do so.

In 1769, Boone set out from North Carolina with a few friends,

Below: "A View of Part of the town of Boston in New England and British Ships of War Landing their Troops 1768." The troops were landing in an attempt to enforce duties and taxes imposed on the colonists. This was one of the acts that infuriated the Americans, and led to their rebellion against the British in 1776.

Above: the colonial settlements had very different patterns of life in different regions. Here a southern plantation is shown, painted by an unknown artist in 1825. These plantations relied mainly on crops of rice and tobacco until the invention of the cotton gin in the late 1700's made cotton the most profitable crop.

and followed the centuries-old "Warriors' Path"—a well-worn Indian route snaking through the dense woods—over the Cumberland Mountains at Cumberland Gap and into Kentucky. Boone was delighted with the richness and wild beauty of the region, and spent two years, often on his own, exploring it. Back in North Carolina, Boone was chosen to lead a group of pioneers over the mountains into Kentucky in 1755. The route he and his party followed soon became known as the "Wilderness Road," and began to be used by countless numbers of pioneer settlers on their way west. Boone himself brought his own family out from North Carolina and settled several miles south of present-day Lexington. But in 1799, he was off again, seeking a new, still-virgin wilderness farther west. For Daniel Boone was a true pioneer, a man driven by a restless spirit of adventure and an irrepressible belief in the opportunities that might lie just over the horizon.

But as the colonists streamed west, blazing trails, clearing fields, and setting up homesteads, they seemed to forget that the lands they were carving out of the wilderness rightfully belonged to another people—the Indians. All along the Atlantic seaboard a single, tragic pattern had emerged from all the contacts between the white men and the native tribes. The Indians' initial friendship and cooperation made it possible for the colonists to survive, but then, as the colony became self-sufficient and began to expand, the colonists rejected the Indians and began driving them out of their lands. Some tribes retreated quietly as their traditional tribal lands were put to the plow. But others fought back, burning and pillaging the British settlements. For such Indians there could be no compromise. They could not accept the white man's insistence on personal property. Their orientation was to communal living and communal property. To them individual ownership of the land was a sacrilege.

But the colonists paid no heed to the Indians' protests. The westward movement was in full swing, and the "heathen natives" must be driven out to make room for the new settlers. Sometimes Indian territories were simply confiscated. Sometimes they were "bought" for a jug of brandy or a few hatchets. Sometimes the colonists bullied and threatened the Indians to make them leave, sometimes they simply massacred them. The most horrible and effective means of eliminating the Indians was the "scalp bounty"—a system by which colonists were paid sums of money for Indian scalps. Any frontiersman in need of cash could easily earn what he needed by scalping a few Indian women and children.

Some of the Indians in eastern and central North America became converts to Christianity, and adopted the white man's way of life. But by doing so, they fired the special hatred of the frontiersmen, who viewed them as a competitive threat. Huddled in European-style villages, such Indians proved an easy prey for murderous white farmers and hostile Indians alike. Those who survived these vicissitudes were cut down by European diseases, to which they were especially vulnerable. The remaining Indians were driven westward. But as they moved away from their traditional lands, their social fabric often disintegrated. The eastern tribes scattered and began to forget their heritage of legends, customs, and beliefs. Even the powerful Iroquois—whose 10,000 warriors had once controlled the giant triangle of land from the Great Lakes and the upper St. Lawrence to the junction of the Ohio and the Mississippi rivers—were ultimately contained and subdued by the thousands of settlers who swarmed west after 1763.

Nothing, it seemed, could stop these new "Americans" once they had set their hearts on going west. Daniel Boone had explained his restless search for virgin lands by saying, "I want more elbow-room!" Many other men felt the same way and, as the fertile river valleys of the east filled up with farms and townships, more and more pioneers pulled up stakes and set out for the wilderness beyond the Appalachian mountains. Many of them began their westward trek on the very rivers that had already played such an important part in the early exploration of America: the St. Lawrence and the Hudson, the Connecticut and the Susquehanna, the Delaware and the James, the Ohio and the Illinois. These and others of the many rivers east of the mighty Mississippi had provided America's first explorers with a gateway to the interior. Now, as they began to provide the pioneers with a stepping-stone to lands yet farther west, these vital waterways more than ever deserved to be called "Rivers of Destiny."

Below: "Daniel Boone Escorting Settlers Through the Cumberland Gap," by George Caleb Bingham. Daniel Boone was typical of many restless American frontiersmen, always pushing over the next line of hills to see what lay in the valley.

Above: Indian chiefs visiting the trustees of Georgia in London, 1734–5. In the early days of several colonies the Indians were treated with respect and many of the early settlers depended heavily on their friendly advice. It was later, when the expanding settlements needed room to grow, that the relationships tended to deteriorate.

Right: "Osceola as a Captive, in a tent Guarded by a Sentry," as painted by Seth Eastman. All too soon the need of the new Americans to move farther west was reason enough for moving the Indians out of the way and ruthlessly punishing any who dared to protest.

America was a land of promise, not only offering the possibility of rich rewards to the explorers, but a fresh start for the hopeful Europeans.

Appendix

Left: Raising of the flag; Louisiana Transfer Ceremonies. The new nation of the United States of America took a great leap westward when Jefferson bought the Louisiana Territory, gaining with it the brave tradition of the Spanish, French, and English men who first took the twisting forest paths and followed the shining rivers into the heart of the unknown continent.

Today, it is hard for us to imagine a time when North America was still an unknown quantity, still a mysterious continent whose very outlines had yet to be mapped. But to America's first explorers, it was just such a land—a "New World" in the truest sense of the words. Before them stretched an uncharted wilderness of vast, silent forests and broad plains, immense lakes and long, winding rivers, strange animals and even stranger peoples. No one knew what might yet be found in the depths of this wilderness. The only certainty was danger, for the New World could be as harsh as it was beautiful. Yet despite its obvious perils, many men found themselves irresistibly drawn to explore it. And, whether they came seeking a Northwest Passage or cities of gold, a fortune in furs or simply greater personal freedom, they all shared a unique spirit of adventure that set them apart from other men.

Nothing captures this spirit of adventure more vividly than the words of the explorers themselves. It is in their writings—and in those of the men who knew and traveled with them—that the true drama of American exploration springs to life. The following pages offer a selection of such firsthand accounts—accounts that provide an exciting, and sometimes surprising, glimpse into the personalities and careers of America's first trailblazers.

Following this selection of contemporary documents there is a brief biographical dictionary of the most important men covered in *Rivers of Destiny*. Most biographies are accompanied by a route map, except in the case of explorers whose journeys have already been mapped earlier in the book.

After the biography section there is a glossary that gives the meaning of unfamiliar words and phrases used in the text. An index and list of picture credits completes the Appendix.

The Medicine Tree

At one time, when the provisions for a long sea voyage consisted chiefly of salt beef and dried biscuits, sailors often developed scurvy, a vitamin-deficiency disease. In this passage from Cartier's account of his second visit to Canada in 1535, he describes the onset of the disease among his men, and the "miraculous" potion that saved them. The tree from which the medicine was made was the white pine, whose leaves and bark are rich in vitamin C.

"In the month of December [1535], we received warning that the pestilence [scurvy] had broken out among the people of Stadacona to such an extent that already, by their own confession, more than fifty persons were dead. Upon this, we forbade them to come either to the fort or about us. But notwithstanding we had driven them away, the sickness broke out among us accompanied by most marvelous and extraordinary symptoms; for some lost all their strength, their legs became swollen and inflamed, while the sinews contracted and turned black as coal. . . . And all had their mouths so tainted [affected], that the gums rotted away down to the roots of the teeth, which nearly all fell out.

"The disease spread among the three ships to such an extent that in the middle of February [1536], of the 110 forming our company, there were not ten in good health so that one could aid the other. . . . Already several had died, whom from sheer weakness, we had to bury beneath the snow; for at that season the ground was frozen and we could not dig into it, so feeble and helpless were we. We were also in great dread of the people of the country, lest they should become aware of our plight and helplessness. And to hide the sickness, our Captain, whom God kept continually in good health, whenever they came near the fort . . . had the sick men hammer and make a noise inside the ships with sticks and stones, pretending that they were caulking. . . .

"We had almost lost hope of ever returning to France, when God in His infinite goodness and mercy had pity on us and made known to us the most excellent remedy against all diseases that has ever been seen or heard of in the whole world. . . . One day our Captain . . . on going outside the fort to walk up and down on the ice, caught sight of a band of Indians approaching from Stadacona, and among them was Domagaia, whom he had seen ten or twelve

Above: Cartier's fleet departs from St. Malo. Scurvy was all too familiar on ships where fresh fruits or vegetables were unknown, and death from the mysterious malady was common.

Below: Cartier setting up the cross with the arms of France to claim the surrounding territory for his king.

days previous to this, extremely ill with the very disease his own men were suffering from. . . . The Captain, seeing Domagaia well and in good health, was delighted, hoping to learn what had healed him, in order to cure his own men. And when the Indians had come near the fort, the Captain inquired of him what had cured him of his sickness. Domagaia replied that he had been healed by the juice of the leaves of a tree. . . . Upon this, the Captain asked him if there was not some of thereabouts, and to show it to him. . . . Thereupon, Domagaia sent two squaws with our Captain to gather some of it. . . . They showed us how to grind the bark and leaves. . . .

"The Captain at once ordered a drink to be prepared for the sick men, but none of them would taste it. At length one or two thought they would risk a trial. . . . After drinking it two or three times, they recovered health and strength and were cured of all the diseases they had ever had. . . . When this became known, there was such a press for the medicine that they almost killed each other to have it first; so that in less than eight days a whole tree as large and as tall as any I ever saw was used up, and produced such a result, that had all the doctors of Louvain and Montpellier been there with all the drugs of Alexandria, they could not have done so much in a year as did this tree in eight days."

The Voyages of Jacques Cartier, *trans. and ed. by H. P. Biggar (Publications of the Public Archives of Canada: Ottawa, 1924) pp. 204–205, 208–209, 212–215.*

Right: Jacques Cartier, who set out to find a northern passage to Asia but discovered the St. Lawrence River instead, the gateway into Canada.

163

Seeking a Way Out of the Wilderness

After De Soto's death in May, 1542, it took the survivors in his party a full year to reach the safety of Spanish Mexico. The travails of their long journey back to civilization are here described by one of the men who took part in the expedition.

"We marched during seventeen days, and arrived at the province of Chavite. . . . We next reached a province called Nisione, and subsequently others called Nandacaho and Lacame. The country becoming more and more barren, the scarcity of provisions increased. . . .

"The cacique [chief] of Nandacaho gave us an Indian for a guide . . . . He then led us into a wild country through which there was no road, and finished by telling us that his master had ordered him to carry us to a place where we should die of hunger. . . .

"Seeing that we were without interpreters and without provisions, and that the maize [corn] which we had brought began to fail—in short, that it was impossible so many persons could travel through so poor a country—we resolved upon returning to the village where the Governor Soto had died, thinking that at that place we should find greater facilities for constructing the vessels in which we might take our departure from the country. . . .

"When we arrived there, we . . . took up our quarters and set to work to build our vessels. Six months were spent in constructing seven brigantines with the utmost difficulty. At length we launched them into the stream, and in truth it was miraculous that they sailed so well and did not let the water in, considering that they were only caulked with the bark of mulberry trees. . . .

"On the second day, as we were descending the river, forty or fifty Indian canoes, of very large size and very light, approached us. One

Above: on almost any forest path there was the possibility of sudden ambush from hostile Indians lying in wait.

Right: the night burial of De Soto, weighted with stones, his body was dropped silently into the Mississippi to keep the Indians from mistreating it.

Above: the desperate survivors flee down the Mississippi River after De Soto's death, under Indian attack.

of these contained eighty warriors, who kept hovering in our rear, and showering their arrows upon us. Many of our men, looking upon it as a piece of cowardice not to attack them, took four or five of our small canoes and advanced against those of the Indians, who, as soon as they saw their maneuvers, surrounded them, cut off their retreat, overturned their canoes, and killed twelve of our best soldiers. . . .

"The Indians, emboldened by their success, continued pursuing us until we reached the sea, which lasted nineteen days. . . . We entered the sea by the mouth of the river, which forms a very large bay. . . . We discovered some small islands on the west side; toward these we shaped our course, and from that time we continually followed the coast . . . till at length we entered the river of Panuco, where we had a welcome reception from the Christians."

A Relation of What Took Place During the Expedition of Captain Soto, *by Luis Hernandez de Biedma, trans. and ed. by William B. Rye (Hakluyt Society: London, 1851) pp. 197-200. Printed with the permission of Cambridge University Press.*

An Encounter with the Great Manito

This story, which records the first meeting between the Indians and Henry Hudson on Manhattan Island in 1609, was told generation after generation by the Algonkians of New York and New Jersey. About 1760, a missionary, John Heckewelder, heard it from the Indians and wrote it down as follows:

"A long time ago, when there was no such thing known to the Indians as people with a white skin . . . some Indians who had gone out a-fishing, and where the the sea widens, espied at a great distance something [Hudson's vessel] swimming or floating on the water, and such as they had never seen before. . . . It was at length agreed . . . that as this phenomenon moved toward the land . . .

Above right: not all of Hudson's contacts with Indians were friendly. Here some of his men attack a village.

Right: Hudson's ship the *Half Moon*, on the first voyage he made for the Dutch East India Company.

it would be well to inform all the Indians on the inhabited islands of what they had seen and put them on their guard.

"Accordingly, they sent runner and watermen off to carry the news to their scattered chiefs, that these might send off in every direction for the warriors to come in. These arriving in numbers, and themselves viewing the strange appearance, and that it was actually moving toward them . . . concluded it to be a large canoe or house, in which the Manito (great or supreme being) himself was, and that he probably was coming to visit them. . . .

"While in this situation, fresh runners arrive, declaring it a house . . . full of people, yet of quite a different color than they [the Indians] are of; that they were also dressed in a different manner from them; and that one in particular appeared altogether [dressed] in red, which must be the Manito himself. They are soon hailed from the vessel, though in a language they do not understand. . . . Many are for running off to the woods, but are pressed to stay, in order not to give offense to their visitors. . . .

"The house (or large canoe, as some will have it) stops, and a smaller canoe comes ashore with the red man and some others in it. . . . The chiefs and wise men . . . have composed a large circle, unto which the red-clothed man with two others approach He salutes them with a friendly countenance, and they return the salute after their manner. . . . He must be the great Manito, they think, but why should he have a white skin?

"A large hockhack [decanter] is brought forward by one of the . . . Manito's servants, and from this a substance is poured out into a small cup . . . and handed to the Manito. The . . . Manito drinks, has the glass filled again, and passes it to the chief next to him to drink. The chief receives the glass, but only smelleth of it, and passes it to the next chief, who does the same.

"The glass thus passes through the circle without the contents being tasted by anyone . . . when one of their number, a spirited man and great warrior, jumps up [and] harangues the assembly on the impropriety of returning the glass with the contents in it: that . . . to return what he [the Manito] had given to them might provoke him . . . and that it was better for one man to die, than a whole nation to be destroyed.

"He then took the glass and, bidding the assembly a farewell, drank it off. Every eye was fixed on their resolute companion to see what effect this would have upon him, and he soon began to stagger about . . . at last dropping on the ground. He falls into a sleep, and they view him as expiring He awakes again, jumps up, and declares that he never felt himself before so happy as after he had drank the cup. Wishes for more. His wish is granted, and the whole assembly joins him and become intoxicated."

Henry Hudson the Navigator: Original Documents, *ed. by G. M. Asher (Hakluyt Society: London, 1860) pp. 174–177. Printed with the permission of Cambridge University Press.*

Smith Among the "Salvages"

Captain John Smith's eleventh-hour rescue by Pocahontas is one of the most famous incidents in American history. Here, Dr. William Simons, a man who was living in Jamestown at the time, tells the story as Smith recounted it to him later.

"To search the country for trade . . . he [Smith] proceeded to the marshes at the river's head, twentie myles in the desert . . . . [Here] he was beset with 200 salvages. Two of them he slew, still defending himself . . . till at last they took him prisoner. . . .

"He demanding for their captain, they shewed him Opechan-kanough . . . to whom he gave a round ivory double compass diall. Much they marvailed at the playing of the . . . needle, which they could see so plainely, and yet not touch it, because of the glass. . . . Notwithstanding, with an houre after, they tyed him to a tree, and as many as could stand about him prepared to shoot him. But the king [Chief Opechankanough] holding up the compass in his hand, they all laid downe their bows and arrows, and in a triumphant manner led him to . . . a long house, where thirtie or fortie tall fellowes did guard him. . . .

"At last they brought him to . . . Powhatan, their emperor. . . .

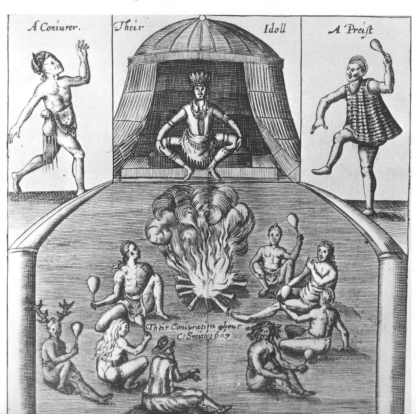

Right: after Captain John Smith had been rescued by Pocahontas, he was adopted by the chief, Powhatan, who gave him an Indian name, "Nantaquod."

Here more than two hundred of those grim courtiers [tribesmen] stood wondering at him [Smith] as he had beene a monster . . . .

"At his entrance before the king . . . a long consultation was held. But the conclusion was, two great stones were brought before Powhatan; then, as many as could laid hands on him, dragged him to them, and thereon laid his head . . . being ready with their clubs to beat out his braines. Pocahontas, the king's dearest daughter, when no entreaty could prevail, got his head in her armes, and laid her owne upon his to save him from death, whereat the emperor was contented he should live. . . .

"Two dayes after, Powhatan . . . came unto him and told him now they were friends, and presently he [Smith] should goe to Jamestown to send him two great gunnes and a gryndestone, for which he would . . . forever exteeme him as his sonne Nantaquod. So to Jamestown with 12 guides Powhatan sent him. . . .

"The next morning betimes they came to the fort, where Smith, having used the salvages with what kindness he could, he shewed Rawhunt, Powhatan's trusty servant, two demi-culverings [small cannon]. . . . But when they [the Indians] did see him discharge them . . . among the boughs of a great tree loaded with isicles, the yce and branches came so tumbling downe that the poor salvages ran away halfe dead with fear. But at last, we regained some conference with them, and gave them such toys, and sent to Powhatan, his women, and children such presents, [as] gave them in general full content."

The Proceedings and Accidents of the English Colony in Virginia, *by William Simons, from The Travels, Adventures, and Observations of Captain John Smith, Vol. 1 (Franklin Press: Richmond, England, 1819) pp. 155, 157–159, 162–163.*

Above: John Smith's experience with Indians by no means ended with the episode in Powhatan's village. Here he takes a chief prisoner in 1608.

Right: John Smith managing to get to shore after the encounter with French pirates on his way to America in 1615.

A Jamestown Colonist Writes Home

Few of the Jamestown settlers possessed John Smith's fortitude and industry. How did the average colonist feel about the hardships of life in Virginia? In the following letter, written from Jamestown in March, 1608, a new arrival named Francis Perkin communicates his hopes and troubles to a friend back in England.

"Illustrious Sir,

After my due commendations to you . . . I am so bold as to beg you once more for a favour. . . . I beg you to be so good as to approach. . . [the members of the Jamestown council] to have me appointed one of the council here in Virginia, not only as an honour to me, but also to enable me the better to pay my debts. There are members of the council who understand affairs of state no better than I do, and whom I equal in business [affairs] . . .

"With regard to our trip over and my opinion of this country, I will inform you as best I can. We left Gravesend [England], Thursday, the eighth of October, 1607. . . . The Ship, called the *John and Francis,* with Captain Christopher Newport, arrived at Jamestown on the second of January. The [James] river is very fair and wide, but full of shoals and oyster-banks. The land is low-lying and forested right down to the coast. . . . The frost was so sharp that I and many others suffered frozen feet. . . .

"After we disembarked, which was on Monday, the following Thursday there was a fire that spread so that all the houses in the fort were burned down, including the storehouse for munitions and supplies. . . . Everything my son and I had was burned, except a mattress which had not yet been taken off the ship.

"Thanks to God, we are at peace with all the inhabitants of the surrounding country, trading for corn and supplies. . . . Their great emperor, or Werowance, which is the name of their kings, has sent some of his people to show us how to plant the native wheat [corn], and to make some gear as they use to go fishing, and surely for all we can guess it is very probable that the land will prove very fertile and good, and extensive enough to accomodate a million people: What we are doing most just now is clearing forests. . . .

"I have sent to my lady your wife a pair of turtle-doves . . . hoping that when our [ships] make another trip I will have better things to send you. . . . There are many little animals here with

Below: Captain Christopher Newport embarks on a trip to investigate the James River, going beyond Jamestown.

Left: providing wives for the settlers was a chronic problem. Here young women land at Jamestown, having been recruited with the promise of a husband in the new Virginia colony.

skins of fine fur. If I come across any I will send them for you and your friends to see. . . .

"I beg you . . . to be so kind as to get Sir William Cornwallis to send me ten pounds of discarded clothing, be it [outer] apparel, underwear, doublet, breeches, mantle, hose, or whatever he likes, for we need everything because the fire burned all we had. . . .

"I am sending to my Lady Catherine [Cornwallis' wife] and to my lady your wife, to each of them six pounds of sassafras to use in medicines or between linnens. . . . I shall not fail to send my Lady Catherine, you, and Sir William Cornwallis some trees, fruit, herbs, flowers, and other new things produced by this land, begging you in the meantime to receive what I can now send in the spirit in which I offer it.

Your servant while he lives,
Francis Perkin. From Jamestown
in Virginia."

The Jamestown Voyages Under the First Charter, 1606–1609, Vol. I, ed. by Philip L. Barbour. (Hakluyt Society: Cambridge, 1969) pp. 158–162. Printed with the permission of Cambridge University Press.

Mutiny at Quebec

Deep in the wilderness, expedition leaders often found themselves faced with serious trouble from their own men. Far from society's laws and regulations, fear, greed, or simple discontent could all too easily turn into a full-scale mutiny. In this passage Champlain describes how one such mutiny began—and ended—at Quebec in 1608.

"Some days after my arrival at Quebec, there was a locksmith [Jean Duval] who conspired . . . to put me to death, and having made himself master of our fort, to hand it over to the Basques or Spaniards. . . . To carry out his wicked plan, hoping thereby to make his fortune, he corrupted four of those whom he considered to be the worst characters, by telling them a host of falsehoods and leading them to hope for gain. After these four had been won over, they all promised to . . . attract the rest to their side. . . .

Below left: the Habitation of Quebec, a reconstruction of the building.

Left: a musketeer of the period. These were the men that formed much of Champlain's expedition.

Below: the Habitation of Quebec as it was illustrated in Champlain's book.

"Being thus all agreed, they made different plans from day to day as to how to kill me in order not to be accused thereof, but this they considered difficult. However . . . they resolved to seize me unarmed and to strangle me, or to give a false alarm at night and to shoot me as I came out. . . . All promised mutually to make no disclosure, on penalty that the first who should open his mouth should be stabbed to death. In four days they were to execute their plan. . . .

"On that same day arrived one of our pinnaces, in which was our pilot, whose name was Captain Testu, a very discreet man. After the pinnace had been unloaded . . . there came to him a locksmith named Natel . . . who told him that he had promised the others to do just the same as they did, but that in reality he did not desire the execution of the plot. . . . The pilot demanded of him that he should disclose the enterprise which they wished to carry out. This Natel did quite fully. The pilot then said to him, 'My good man, you have done well to divulge such a wicked scheme . . . but these things must not go on without the Sieur de Champlain being told, in order that he may take measures against them. . . .'

"The pilot came at once to me in a garden which I was having made, and said that he desired to speak to me privately. . . . We went into the wood, where he related to me the whole affair. . . . He begged me to pardon the man who had told him, to which I consented, although he ought to have come to me. I told him that I was better able to control myself in such affairs, and that he was to bring the man so that I might hear his tale. He went, and brought him all trembling with fear lest I should do him some harm. . . .

"After hearing him and questioning him, I told him to go about his work. . . . Then I gave two bottles of wine to a young fellow and directed him to tell these four worthy ringleaders of the undertaking that it was wine which his friends at Tadoussac had given him as a present and that he wanted to share it with them. They did not decline the invitation, and toward evening went on board the pinnace where he was to offer them the refreshment. I was not long in following them, and ordered them to be seized.

"There then were my gentry [other men] properly astonished. I at once made everyone get up, though it was nearly ten o'clock in the evening, and forgave them all, on condition that they should tell the truth about everything. This they did. . . .

Mutiny at Quebec

"On the following day I received all their depositions [statements], one after the other, in the presence of the pilot and of the sailors of the ship, and had them committed to writing. And they were very glad . . . for they were living in constant fear of one another, and particularly of the four scoundrels who had misled them. . . . When this had been done, I took my fine fellows off to Tadoussac, and begged Pont-Gravé to do me the favor of guarding them . . . as I had not yet any safe place to put them in, and we were much occupied with the construction of our houses [at Quebec]. . . .

"Some time after this we had them confronted, and all that had been stated . . . was reaffirmed, without any denial on the part of the prisoners, who confessed that they had acted wickedly and deserved punishment. . . . We decided that it would be sufficient to put to death Duval as the first mover in the conspiracy, and also to serve as an example to those who remained to behave properly in future. . . . Duval was hanged . . . at Quebec . . . and the other three were sent back to France."

The Works of Samuel de Champlain, Vol. II, *trans. by John Squair* (*The Champlain Society: Toronto, 1925*) *pp. 25–34.*

Below: a fort of the Iroquois Indians. Champlain was a brave and valiant fighter, and it was his friendship with the Huron Indians that led him to take their part in the battle with the Iroquois—thus winning persistent Iroquois enmity against the French.

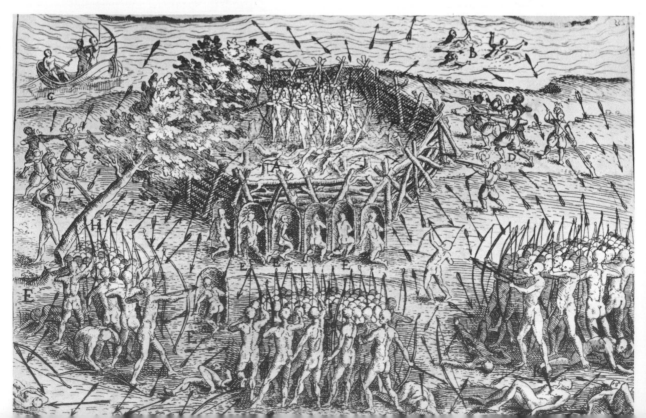

On to the Great Lakes

Right: the buffalo was an important animal to the Indians and a fascinating one to the Europeans—this early view of one is from Father Hennepin's book.

When Radisson and Groseilliers set out for the Great Lakes in 1659, they were accompanied by 31 other Frenchmen. But by the time they had got as far as the Ottawa River rapids their companions had lost their nerve, given up, and left for home. Radisson here describes their departure, and touches on some of the things he saw as he and his brother-in-law continued their journey alone.

"The French . . . resolved to give an end to such labors and dangers. . . . We [Radisson and Groseilliers] kept still our resolution . . . that we would finish that voyage or die by the way. . . . After long arguing . . . all with one consent went back and we went on. . . .

"We embarked ourselves on the delightfullest lake of the world [Lake Huron]. . . . The country was so pleasant, so beautifull and fruitfull, that it grieved me to see that the world could not discover such inticing countrys to live in. . . .

"We came to the strait of the 2 lakes [Sault Ste. Marie]. . . . There we passed the winter . . . and killed staggs [deer], buffes [buffalo], elends [moose], and castors [beaver]. . . . The snow proved favorable that year, which caused much plenty of everything. Most of the woods and forests are very thick, so that in some places it was as dark as in a cellar. . . . As for the buff, it is a furious animal. One must have a care of him, for every year he kills some Nadoueseronons [Indians]. He comes for the most part in the plains and meddows. He feeds like an ox . . . he hath a very long tail: he is reddish, his hair frizzed and very fine."

Radisson's Account of His Third Journey, *from Early Narratives of the Northwest, ed. by Louise Phelps Kellog (Charles Scribners Sons: New York, 1917) pp. 40, 47, 50–52.*

Marquette Meets the Illinois

Above: Father Jacques Marquette. Fluent in several Indian languages, he was an asset to Joliet on the expedition.

Below: smoking the pipe of peace. For many Indian tribes, smoking was a ceremonial act, often used to signify peace and friendship between tribes.

Like many of the Jesuit priests who came to America to work among the Indians, Father Marquette was a man of great courage as well as sincere dedication. In the following passage, he describes the tense moments leading up to his first encounter with the Illinois Indians during his and Joliet's historic trip down the Mississippi.

"Here we are then, on this so-renowned river [the Mississippi]. . . . We continued to advance but, as we knew not whither we were going—for we had proceeded over one hundred leagues [about 350 miles] without discovering anything except animals and birds— we kept well on our guard. On this account, we make only a small fire on land toward evening . . . and, after supper, we remove ourselves as far from it as possible and pass the night in our canoes. . . .

"Finally, on the 25th of June, we perceived on the water's edge some tracks of men, and a narrow and somewhat beaten path leading to a fine prairie. We stopped to examine it and, thinking that it was a road which led to some village of savages, we resolved to go and reconnoiter it. . . . Monsieur Jollyet and I undertook this investigation—a rather hazardous one for two men who exposed themselves, alone, to the mercy of a barbarous and unknown people.

"We silently followed the narrow path and, after walking about two leagues [almost seven miles], we discovered a village. . . . We went farther without being perceived, and approached so near that we could even hear the savages talking. We therefore decided that it was time to reveal ourselves. This we did by shouting with all our energy, and stopped, without advancing any farther.

"On hearing the shout, the savages quickly issued from their cabins and . . . deputed [appointed] four old men to come and speak to us. Two of these bore tobacco-pipes, finely ornamented and adorned with various feathers. They walked slowly, and raised their pipes to the sun . . . without, however, saying a word. . . . Finally, when they had drawn near, they stopped to consider us attentively. I was reassured when I observed these ceremonies, which with them are performed only among friends. . . . I therefore spoke to them first, and asked them who they were. They replied that they were Illinois, and . . . invited us to enter their village. . . .

Above: Marquette and Joliet during the trip down the Mississippi. For the devout Jesuits, the chance of reaching Indians not yet acquainted with the Christian faith was more important than mapping the unknown territories.

"At the door of the cabin in which we were to be received was an old man, who awaited us . . . with his hands extended and lifted to the sun. . . . When we came near him, he paid us this compliment: 'How beautiful the sun is, O Frenchmen, when thou comest to visit us. All our village awaits thee, and thou shalt enter all our cabins in peace! Having said this, he made us enter his own. . . .

"After we had taken our places, the usual civility of the country was paid to us, which consisted in offering us the calumet [peace pipe]. This must not be refused, unless one wishes to be considered an enemy, or at least uncivil. . . . While all the elders smoked after us, in order to do us honor, we received an invitation on behalf of the great captain of all the Illinois to proceed to his village, where he wished to hold a council with us. We went thither in a large company, for all these people, who had never seen any Frenchmen among them, could not cease looking at us. They lay on the grass along the road; they preceded us, and then retraced their steps to come and see us again All this was done noiselessly, and with marks of great respect for us."

The Mississippi Voyage of Joliet and Marquette, 1673, *from Early Narratives of the Northwest, ed. by Louise Phelps Kellog (Charles Scribners Sons: New York, 1917) pp. 236, 238–240.*

An Unpreventable Death

Above: Robert Cavelier, Sieur de La Salle, who followed the Mississippi River south to the Gulf of Mexico.

In 1669, La Salle, then aged 26, embarked on a daring expedition in search of the Ohio River. With him—as far as Lake Ontario—went two young priests named Dollier and Galinée. All three spoke Algonkian, but not Iroquois, a deficiency that prevented them from saving a life early on in their journey. The incident is described in the following passage, written by Galinée.

"M. de La Salle had long been premeditating [a journey] toward a great river . . . called, in the language of the Iroquois 'Ohio'. . . . The hope of beaver, but especially of finding by this route the passage into the Vermillion Sea [Gulf of California], into which M. de La Salle believed the River Ohio emptied, induced him to undertake this expedition, so as not to leave to another the honor of discovering . . . the way to China. . . .

"M. de La Salle, who said that he understood the Iroquois [language] perfectly . . . did not know it at all, and was embarking upon this expedition almost blindly, scarcely knowing where he was going. He had been led to expect that by making some present to the village of the Seneca [Iroquois], he could readily procure slaves . . . who might serve him as guides. As for myself, I would not start . . . unless I could take with me a man who knew Iroquois. . . . The only person I could find who could serve me for this purpose was a Dutchman. . . . He knows Iroquois perfectly, but French very little. . . .

"We left Montreal on the 6th of July and . . . after thirty-five days of very difficult navigation, we arrived at a small stream . . . about one hundred leagues [almost 350 miles] southwestward from Montreal. . . . No sooner had we arrived at this place than we were visited by a number of [Seneca] Indians who . . . told us we were expected at the village, and that word had been sent through all the cabins to assemble all the old men for the council, which was to be held to learn the reason of our coming. . . . Thereupon, an Indian . . . took us to the largest cabin of the village. . . .

"The Indians assembled in our cabin to the number of fifty or sixty of the principal persons of the nation. . . . When we saw the assembly was numerous enough, we began to talk business, and it was then that M. de La Salle admitted he was unable to make himself understood. . . . Our interpreter . . . told us they [the Seneca] would give us a slave, as we had asked for one, but begged us to

Below: the cruelty of the Iroquois, from Father Louis Hennepin's book. The tortures that Indian tribes were in the habit of practicing on captives horrified the European explorers.

wait until their people came back from the trade with the Dutch, to which they had taken all their slaves, and then they would give us one without fail. . . . Meanwhile, they treated us in the best way they could, and everyone vied with his neighbor in feasting us after the fashion of the country. . . .

"It was during that time that I saw the saddest spectacle I ever saw in my life. I was told one evening that some warriors had arrived, that they had brought in a prisoner, and he had been put in a cabin not far from our own. . . . They . . . had done him no harm since his capture; they had not even given him the salutation of blows with sticks which it is their custom to give prisoners on entering the village. So I thought I should have time to ask for him in order that he might be our guide. . . .

"Night came on and we went to bed. The light of next day had no sooner appeared than a large company entered our cabin to tell us the prisoner was to be burned. . . . I ran to the public square to see him, and found him already on the scaffold, where they were fastening him hand and foot to the stake. . . . The irons were in the fire to torture the poor wretch. . . .

"I told my interpreter to ask for him as the slave that had been promised . . . but our interpreter never would make this proposition, saying it was not the custom amongst them, and the matter was too important. I went so far as to threaten him in order to say what I wished, but could effect nothing, because he was obstinate like a Dutchman, and ran away from me. . . .

A
JOURNAL
Of the LAST
VOYAGE
Perform'd by
Monfr. de la Sale,
TO THE
GULPH of MEXICO,
To find out the
Mouth of the *Miſſiſipi* River;
CONTAINING,
An Account of the Settlements he endeavour'd to make on the Coaſt of the aforeſaid *Bay*, his unfortunate Death, and the Travels of his Companions for the Space of Eight Hundred Leagues acroſs that Inland Country of *America*. now call'd *Louiſiana*, (and given by the King of *France* to M. *Crozat*,)till they came into *Canada*.
Written in French *by Monſieur* JOUTEL,
A Commander in that Expedition;
And Tranſlated from the Edition juſt publiſh'd at Paris.
With an exaſt Map of that vaſt Country, and a Copy of the *Letters Patents* granted by the K. of *France* to M. *Crozat*.
LONDON, Printed for *A. Bell* at the *Croſs-Keys* and *Bible* in Cornbill, *B. Lintott* at the *Croſs Keys* in *Fleet-ſtreet*, and *J. Baker* in *Pater-Noſter-Row*, 1714.

Above: the title page of the English translation of Joutel's book, telling of La Salle's attempt to establish a colony at the mouth of the Mississippi River to strengthen the French claim.

An Unpreventable Death

"I retired therefore with grief, and scarcely had I turned my head when this barbarian of an Iroquois applied his red-hot gun barrel to the top of his [the captive's] feet, which made the poor wretch utter a loud cry, and forced me to turn toward him. I saw that Iroquois with a grave and steady hand applying the iron slowly along his feet and legs, and . . . all the young people leaping for joy to see the contortions that the violence of the fire compelled the poor sufferer to make.

"Meanwhile, I retired to the cabin in which we lodged, filled with grief at not being able to save this poor slave, and it was then that I recognized more than ever how important it was not to engage oneself amongst the tribes of these countries without knowing their language or being sure of one's interpreter."

The Journey of Dollier and Galinée, 1669–1670, *from Early Narratives of the Northwest, ed. by Louise Phelps Kellog (Charles Scribners Sons: New York, 1917) pp. 168, 171, 177–185.*

Right: Henri de Tonti, the great friend of La Salle, who went with him on many of his expeditions into the interior.

Below left: one continual difficulty of early life in the colonies was that the settlers had to supply themselves for any eventuality. Here La Salle supervises the unloading of a ship.

Below: the explorers had to learn to live off the land, eating whatever kind of meat they could find. Here La Salle's men shoot a bear swimming in the river.

The Murder of La Salle

La Salle's loyal friend and brave lieutenant, Henri de Tonti, was not with him on his last, ill-fated expedition to the Gulf of Mexico. Tonti was commanding the fort at St. Louis in 1687 when he learned of La Salle's tragic death in Texas. Here, Tonti recounts the story of the murder as it was reported to him.

"M. de La Salle, having landed beyond the Mississippy . . . and having lost his vessels on the coast . . . began to march along the seashore in search of the Mississippy . . . Finding himself short of provisions, he sent M. de Morangé, his servant, and the Chaouanon [Indian guide] to hunt in a small wood, with orders to return in the evening. When they had killed some buffaloes, they stopped to dry the meat. M. de La Salle was uneasy, so he asked the Frenchmen who among them would go and look for them?

"De Haut and Lanquetot [two other members of the party] had for a long time determined to kill M. de La Salle . . . and, as in a long journey there are always discontented persons in a company, he [Lanquetot] easily found partisans. He offered therefore, with them, to go in search of M. de Morangé, in order to have an opportunity to execute their design.

"Having found the men, he told them M. de La Salle was uneasy about them; but they [Lanquetot and Du Haut] declaring that they could not set off until the next day, it was agreed to sleep there. After supper they arranged the order of the watch: that it should begin with M. de Morangé; after him was to follow the servant of M. de La Salle; and then the Chaouanon. After they had kept their watch and were asleep, the others massacred them as persons attached to M. de La Salle.

"Toward daybreak, they heard the reports of pistols, which were fired as signals by M. de La Salle, who was coming . . . in search of them. The wretches, suspecting that it was he, lay in wait for him. . . . As M. de La Salle advanced . . . he received three balls [bullets] in the head, and fell down dead. . . . Such was the end of one of the greatest men of this age, a man of an admirable spirit, and capable of undertaking all sorts of explorations."

Memoir on La Salle's Discoveries, by Tonty, 1678–1690, *from Early Narratives of the Northwest, ed. by Louise Phelps Kellog (Charles Scribners Sons: New York, 1917) pp. 317–319.*

The Explorers

AMADAS, PHILIP
1550–1618   England
1584: On a voyage for Sir Walter
Raleigh, sailed, with Arthur Barlowe, to
the shores of North Carolina. Explored
Pamlico Sound and Roanoke Island.
1585: Accompanied Raleigh's first
group of colonists to Roanoke.
See map on page 96.

BAFFIN, WILLIAM
1584–1622   England
1612: Took part in an expedition to
Greenland.
1615: Sailed with Robert Bylot in
search of the Northwest Passage.
Traveled through Hudson Strait into
Hudson Bay. Gave his name to the large
island on the northern side of Hudson
Strait.
1616: Again with Bylot, made a second
attempt to find the Northwest Passage.
Explored Baffin Bay and discovered
several sounds leading into the Arctic
Ocean. These he named Jones, Smith,
and Lancaster sounds.
See map on page 120.

BARLOWE, ARTHUR
1550(?)–1620   England
1584: With Philip Amadas, explored the
coast of North Carolina for Sir Walter
Raleigh. It was Barlowe's glowing
report of Roanoke Island that led
Raleigh to choose it as the site of his
proposed colony.
See map on page 96.

BLOCK, ADRIAEN
dates unknown   The Netherlands
1614: Journeyed to the mouth of the
Hudson on a fur-trading expedition.
Explored the Connecticut coastline and
the Connecticut River Valley, which he
claimed for the Dutch.
See map on page 120.

BOONE, DANIEL
1734–1820   Pennsylvania
1755: Took part in General Braddock's
attempt to seize Fort Duquesne (now
Pittsburgh) from the French.
1769: Set off from North Carolina, and
followed the "Warriors' Path" through
the Cumberland Mountains at

Cumberland Gap and into Kentucky.
Explored the region extensively before
returning home.
1775: Led a group of woodsmen and
settlers west to improve and connect
existing Indian trails into Kentucky.
This became the "Wilderness Trail."
Built a fort (Boonesborough) at the
end of Boone's Trace (an offshoot of
the Wilderness Road) several miles
from present-day Lexington.
1799: Set out for unexplored territory
again, and traveled to the Femme Osage
district, about 40 miles from present-
day St. Louis, Missouri.

BRULÉ, ETIENNE
1592(?)–1633   France
1608: Traveled to Quebec with
Champlain.
1610: Chosen by Champlain to spend a
year with an Algonkian tribe in southern
Ontario. While with them, traveled west
to Lake Huron.
1618–1629: Lived and traveled with
the Huron Indians collecting furs for
the French. During this time (probably
in 1620), explored the Upper Michigan
Peninsula.
See map on pages 78-79

BYLOT, ROBERT
dates unknown   England
See Baffin, William

CABEZA DE VACA, ÁLVAR NÚÑEZ
1490(?)–1557(?)   Spain
1528: Took part in Pánfilo de Narváez'
ill-fated expedition into Florida. Was
one of those who survived the

expedition's shipwreck in the Gulf of
Mexico.
1529–1535: Lived as a captive of an
Indian tribe along the Texas coast.
1536: With a few companions,
managed to escape from the Indians
and reach Spanish Mexico by traveling
overland.
1540: Became governor of Paraguay.
Discovered Iguaçu Falls in Brazil.
See map on pages 50-51

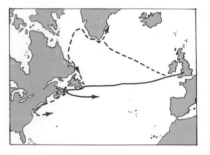

CABOT, JOHN
1450–1498   Venice
1497: In the service of England, sailed
west in search of Asia. Made a landing
on either Newfoundland or Nova
Scotia, and claimed the region for
England. Returned home after sailing
south and west around Cape Breton
Island.
1498: Explored east and west coasts of
Greenland. Followed the Labrador
coast to Nova Scotia and then sailed
southward, possibly even reaching
Delaware Bay before starting back.

CADILLAC, ANTOINE
DE LA MOTHE
1656(?)–1730   France
1683: Emigrated to New France and
lived in Nova Scotia and Maine.
1694: Received command of Mackinac,
Michigan, then the most important
fur-trading post in the west.
1701: Founded a colony at Detroit,
Michigan.
1711: Became governor of Louisiana.

CARDENAS, GARCÍA LÓPEZ DE
dates unknown   Spain
1540–1542: Took part in Coronado's
expedition into the Southwest. Headed

a small exploring party that discovered the Grand Canyon.
See map on pages 50-51

CARTIER, JACQUES
1491–1557   France
1534: Sailed westward in search of the Northwest Passage. Reached Newfoundland, then traveled through the Strait of Belle Isle and across the Gulf of St. Lawrence to Gaspé Peninsula.
1535: Sailed west again, and discovered the mouth of the St. Lawrence. Sailed up the river to present-day Montreal. Sighted and named the Lachine Rapids.
1541: Voyaged to America again, still searching unsuccessfully for the Northwest Passage.
See map on pages 78-79

CHAMPLAIN, SAMUEL DE
1567(?)–1635   France
1599–1601: Sailed to the West Indies and Central America for Spain.
1603: Accompanied an expedition to New France. Traveled up the St. Lawrence River to present-day Montreal.
1604: Accompanied another expedition, this time to Nova Scotia, where he helped found Port Royal. Explored and mapped the New England coastline from Maine to Cape Cod.
1608: Sailed to New France again, and founded Quebec.
1609: Accompanied a Huron war party into upstate New York and discovered Lake Champlain.
1613: In search of a water route to Asia, traveled up the Ottawa River to Lake Nipissing.
1615: With an Algonkian war party, traveled west to Georgia Bay on Lake Huron, and southeast to Lake Oneida in southern New York state.
1620: Sent Étienne Brulé to explore the Upper Michigan Peninsula.
1633: Became governor of New France.
1634: Sent Jean Nicolet to explore the western shores of Lake Michigan.
See map on pages 78-79

CORONADO, FRANCISCO VÁSQUEZ DE
1510–1554   Spain
1538: Became governor of New Galicia near Mexico City.
1540–1542: Led an expedition into the American Southwest in search of the Seven Cities of Cibola. Journeyed through Arizona, New Mexico, and central Kansas. Some of his men discovered the Grand Canyon.
See map on pages 50-51

DE SOTO, HERNANDO
1500(?)–1542   Spain
1519–1521: Took part in the Spanish conquest of the Inca Empire.

1538: Became governor of Cuba.
1539–1540: Led an expedition into the American South in search of the Seven Cities of Cibola. Traveled north through Florida into Georgia. Explored Blue Ridge mountains. Crossed into Alabama, and then traveled northwest through Mississippi.
1541: Sighted the Mississippi River near the site of present-day Memphis, Tennessee. Crossed into Arkansas, and explored the Ozark mountains.
1542: Returned to the Mississippi River in northeastern Louisiana, where he fell sick and died.
See map on pages 50-51

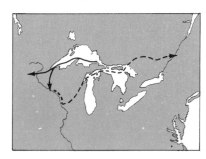

DULUTH, SIEUR, DANIEL GREYSOLON
1636–1710   France
1678–1680: Traveled to the Lake Superior region. Rescued Father Hennepin from the Sioux Indians. Explored the headwaters of the Mississippi River, and claimed all the surrounding territory for France.

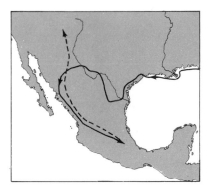

ESTEVANICO
dates unknown   Morocco
1528: Took part in Pánfilo de Narváez' expedition to Florida. Was among the survivors of the expedition after a shipwreck in the Gulf of Mexico.
1529–1534: Lived as a captive of an Indian tribe on the Texas coast.
1536: With Cabeza de Vaca and two others, escaped from captivity and reached New Spain.
1539: Sent, with Fray Marcos de Niza, into the Southwest on a reconnaissance mission to gather information about the

Seven Cities of Cibola. Was killed by Zuñi Indians in New Mexico.

FROBISHER, SIR MARTIN
1535(?)–1594   England
1576: Sailed west to find the Northwest Passage. Rounded Greenland, visited Labrador, and discovered Frobisher Bay on Baffin Island.
1577: Sailed west again, revisiting many of the places he had seen before.
1578: Sailed west into Hudson Strait.
See map on page 120

GILBERT, SIR HUMPHREY
1539(?)–1583   England
1578: Sailed west in search of the Northwest Passage.
1583: Set out once more and reached Newfoundland, where he set up a colony near present-day St. John's.
See map on page 96

GOSNOLD, BARTHOLOMEW
(?)–1607   England
1602: Explored coastlines of Maine and Massachusetts. Discovered Martha's Vineyard.
1607: Second in command of colonizing expedition to Jamestown.
See map on page 96

GRENVILLE, SIR RICHARD
1541–1591   England
1585: Commanded Raleigh's first colonizing expedition to Virginia.
See map on page 96

GROSEILLIERS, SIEUR DE, MÉDART CHOUART
1625(?)–1697   France
1654–1657: Traveled to Green Bay on the western shores of Lake Michigan, and explored Sault Ste. Marie.
1659–1660: With Pierre Ésprit Radisson, traveled again to Sault Ste. Marie. This time continued westward along the southern shores of Lake Superior to Chequamegon Bay.
1661: With Radisson, reached the extreme western tip of Lake Superior. Traveled into present-day Minnesota, and then turned northward, traveling overland and by canoe to Hudson Bay.
1665: Quarreled with the French authorities and, with Radisson, entered the service of England.
1668: In the course of expeditions for England, established fur-trading post at Hudson Bay. The success of this post led to the founding of England's Hudson's Bay Company.
See map on page 148

HENNEPIN, FATHER LOUIS
1640(?)–1701(?)   Belgium
1678: Accompanied La Salle to the Niagara River. There, became the first white man to draw and describe Niagara Falls. Supervised the building

of the *Griffin* while La Salle traveled back to Fort Frontenac to gather supplies.
1679: Sailed with La Salle from Lake Erie to Lake Michigan. Accompanied La Salle to the Illinois River, and helped in the building of Fort Crèvecoeur near present-day Peoria. Was sent by La Salle to explore the lower reaches of the Illinois. Was captured by a party of Sioux Indians.
1680: Rescued from the Indians by Sieur Duluth, and subsequently returned to Europe.
See map on page 148

HUDSON, HENRY
(?)–1611   England
1607: In the service of the English Muscovy Company, sought a northeast passage to the Orient.
1608: Sailed northeast again, this time reaching Novaya Zemlya.
1609: Sailed to North America in the service of the Dutch East India Company. Entered New York harbor and explored the Hudson River north-ward to present-day Albany.
1610–1611: In the service of England, sailed west in search of the Northwest Passage. Discovered Hudson Strait and Hudson Bay. Was cast adrift by his mutinous crew in James Bay.
See map on page 120

JOLIET, LOUIS
1645–1700   Canada
1669: Sent west by colonial authorities to carry supplies to a French expedition near Lake Superior.
1673: Traveled, with Father Jacques Marquette, from St. Ignace on Lake Michigan, to the Mississippi, and down the Mississippi to the mouth of the Arkansas River. Here, having deter-mined that the Mississippi emptied out into the Gulf of Mexico, turned back to make his report in Montreal.
1674: Was granted the island of Anticosti for his exploratory work.
1697: Explored the Hudson Bay area for the French authorities.
See map on page 148

LA SALLE, SIEUR DE, ROBERT CAVELIER
1643–1687   France
1666: Traveled to New France to seek his fortune.
1669: In search of the Ohio River, traveled with two missionaries down the St. Lawrence and into upstate New York. Near the southern end of Lake Ontario left the missionaries and set out for the interior alone. Located the Ohio River, which he followed as far as present-day Louisville, Kentucky. Continuing northward, crossed Lake Michigan, and explored the Illinois River Valley.

1674: Was granted a tract of land near present-day Kingston, Ontario which included Fort Frontenac.
1678: Set out for the Niagara River with the idea of building a sailing ship to navigate the Great Lakes.
1679: Upon completion of the ship, the *Griffin,* sailed west through Lake Ontario, Lake Erie, and Lake Huron to the southern shores of Lake Michigan. Sent the ship back with orders to return with supplies for a journey down the Mississippi. Traveled to the Illinois River and built Fort Crèvecoeur on the site of present-day Peoria, Illinois.
1680: Receiving no word of the *Griffin*'s return, set out to discover its fate. Traveled to the mouth of the St. Joseph River, then northeast to Niagara and Fort Frontenac. Learning there that his men had mutinied at Fort Crèvecoeur, set out to find his lieutenant, Henri de Tonti.
1681: Reunited with Tonti in Wisconsin. Organized an expedition and set out down the Illinois to explore the Mississippi.
1682: Traveled the length of the Mississippi River, reaching the Gulf coast in April. Claimed the entire Mississippi Valley for France, and then returned to the St. Lawrence, pausing along the Illinois River to build Fort St. Louis. Traveled to France to request a large expedition to found a colony on the Gulf coast.
1684: Sailed from France with several ships bound for the mouth of the Mississippi River. Failed to locate the river's main channel and landed at Matagorda Bay, Texas.
1687: After many fruitless attempts to locate the Mississippi, was killed by his own men near the Brazos River.
See map on page 148

MARQUETTE, FATHER JACQUES
1637–1675   France
1666: Traveled to New France to work and teach among the Ottawa Indians.
1671: Founded a mission called St. Ignace on the northern shore of the Strait of Mackinac.
1673: With Louis Joliet, traveled down the Mississippi to the Arkansas River. There, having determined that the Mississippi emptied into the Gulf of Mexico, began the return trip to the Great Lakes.
1674–1675: Worked among Illinois tribes.
See map on page 148.

MOSCOSO, DE ALVARADO, LUIS DE
dates unknown   Spain
1519–1521: Took part in the Spanish conquest of Central America.
1539: Set out with De Soto's expedition to explore the American South.

1542: After De Soto's death, led the expedition from northeastern Louisiana overland into Texas. Returned to the Mississippi River in Louisiana and built boats in which his men floated down the Mississippi and crossed the Gulf of Mexico to Spanish Mexico.
See map on pages 50-51

NARVÁEZ, PÁNFILO DE
1478(?)–1528   Spain
1511: Took part in the Spanish conquest of Cuba.
1521: Was sent to arrest Cortes in Mexico, but was surprised by Cortes ir Veracruz and imprisoned for two years.
1526: Was granted the unexplored regions of Florida.
1527: Led an expedition deep into the Florida wilderness in search of the Seven Cities of Cibola.
1528: Returned to the Florida coast to find that his ships had gone. Built crude boats to sail to New Spain via Gulf of Mexico. Was drowned when his boat capsized in the Gulf.
See map on pages 50-51

NICOLET, JEAN
1598–1642   France
1618: Brought to New France by Champlain, and went to live with the Algonkian Indians to learn their language and customs.
1634: For Champlain, traveled to Green Bay on Lake Michigan, where he met the Winnebago Indians.
See map on pages 78-79

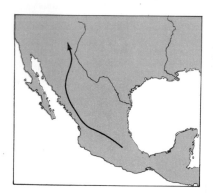

NIZA, FRAY MARCOS DE
(?)–1558   Italy
1539: In the service of Spain, explored parts of Arizona and western New Mexico with a Moroccan named Estevanico. After Estevanico's death, returned to New Spain and falsely reported that he had seen "cities of gold and silver."
1540: Accompanied Coronado's expedition into the American Southwest.

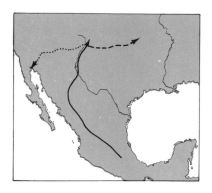

OÑATE, JUAN DE

1549(?)–1628(?)   Spain
1598: Led an expedition to conquer and colonize the New Mexico region. Founded a settlement at an Indian pueblo near the Chama River.
1601: Sent exploring parties into Kansas.
1605: Sent exploring parties to the Gulf of California.

PONCE DE LEÓN, JUAN

1460(?)–1521   Spain
1493: Took part in Columbus' second voyage to America.
1508: Conquered Puerto Rico. There, Indians told him of an island called Bimini, where there was supposed to be a fountain that restored youth.
1513: Set out in search of Bimini, and discovered a large landmass that he named "Florida." Explored both its east and west coasts.
1521: Unsuccessfully attempted to found a colony in Florida.
See map on pages 50-51

RADDISSON, PIERRE ÉSPRIT

1636(?)–1710(?)   France
1652–1654: Lived as a captive of the Iroquois in upstate New York.
1654: Took part in a Jesuit expedition into the heart of Iroquois territory.
1659–1660: With his brother-in-law, Sieur de Groseilliers, traveled to Sault Ste. Marie and paddled along the southern shores of Lake Superior to Chequamegon Bay.
1661: Again with Groseilliers, traveled to the extreme western tip of Lake Superior. Journeyed a short distance into present-day Minnesota, then headed north, traveling as far as the Hudson Bay area.
1665: Quarreled with the French authorities and offered his services to England.
1668: Made several trips to Hudson Bay region for England to establish fur-trading posts.
1670: As a result of his and Groseillier's work, the English founded the Hudson's Bay Company.
See map on page 148

SMITH, JOHN

1580–1631   England
1595–1604: Traveled extensively in Europe as a mercenary soldier. Was captured by the Turks and sent to Russia as a slave.
1607: Sailed with the first Jamestown colonists to Virginia. Led exploring parties up the Potomac and Rappahannock rivers and around Chesapeake Bay. Played a vital role in establishing good relations between colonists and Powhatan Indians.
1608: Became president of Jamestown, and forced colonists to work hard to save themselves from starvation.
1609: Wounded in a gunpowder accident. Returned to England.
1614: Sailed to America for Sir Ferdinando Gorges and explored the coast from Cape Cod to Penobscot Bay. Named this part of the Atlantic seaboard "New England."
1615: Sailed with a group of colonists bound for Massachusetts Bay. Captured by French pirates. While in captivity, made a detailed map of the New England coastline, which was later used by the Pilgrims.
See map on page 96

TONTI, HENRI DE

1650–1704   France
1678: Went to Canada with La Salle.
1679: Accompanied La Salle to Niagara where he helped build the *Griffin.* Sailed with La Salle from Lake Erie to Lake Michigan. Traveled with him to Illinois River and helped build Fort Crèvecoeur near modern Peoria.
1680–1681: Left in charge of Fort Crèvecoeur while La Salle went east. His men mutinied and he was captured by the Iroquois. On being released, made his way to Wisconsin, where he was finally reunited with La Salle.
1682: Accompanied La Salle down the Mississippi River to the Gulf of Mexico. Traveled back with La Salle up the Mississippi River and helped build Fort St. Louis at Starved Rock, Illinois.
1684–1687: Commanded Fort St. Louis while awaiting La Salle, who planned to voyage up the Mississippi and thence up the Illinois from the Gulf of Mexico. Learning of La Salle's death, made an unsuccessful attempt to rescue the stranded members of La Salle's expedition still at Matagorda Bay, Texas.
1687–1699: Worked in Illinois region helping to establish French outposts and settlements.
1702: Joined French-Canadian explorer Sieur d'Iberville in Louisiana.
See map on page 148

VERRAZANO, GIOVANNI DA

1485(?)–1527(?)   Florence

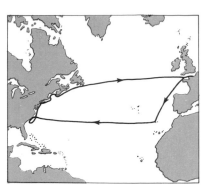

1524: In the service of Francis I of France, sailed to America. Reached North Carolina and then sailed north, possibly even reaching Nova Scotia and Newfoundland. During the voyage, explored New York harbor and the mouth of the Hudson River.

WAYMOUTH, GEORGE

dates unknown   England
1605: Sailed to the shores of New England for Sir Ferdinando Gorges and Sir John Popham. Followed coast northward from Nantucket Sound to the mouth of the Kennebec River, which he explored before returning home.
See map on page 96

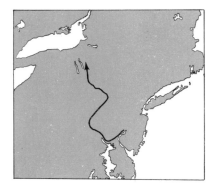

WEISER, CONRAD

dates unknown   Pennsylvania
1736: Sent from Philadelphia on a peace mission to the Iroquois. Despite heavy snows, broke a trail through the wilderness to Onondaga, where he succeeded in arranging a peace treaty with the Iroquois.

WHITE, JOHN

dates unknown   England
1587: For Sir Walter Raleigh, sailed to Roanoke with 117 colonists.
1588: Took part in English sea battle against the Spanish Armada.
1590: Returned to Roanoke with supplies, only to find that the entire colony had vanished without trace.
See map on page 96

Glossary

armada: Any large fleet of well-armed vessels. Often refers to the Spanish or "Invincible" Armada built by Philip II of Spain, which was defeated by the English in 1588.

bayou: A small curving channel that drains a larger river or swamp. The term is chiefly used in the Mississippi basin and Gulf-coast regions.

brigantine: A two-masted, square-rigged sailing vessel.

buccaneers: The name given to the English, French, and Dutch sea rovers who made their living by pirating Spanish vessels laden with New World gold and silver. The buccaneers operated chiefly in the West Indies, through which most of the treasure ships had to pass on their way back to Spain.

cacique: The name used by the Spanish conquistadors when referring to the chief of an Indian tribe.

charter: An official document issued by a monarch or government to grant certain rights, privileges, or powers to an individual or group. The early explorers and colonists had to obtain charters before setting off to explore or establish a colony in America.

conquistadors: The Spanish soldiers and adventurers who came to the New World in the 1500's to seek their fortune. Their hopes of gold and glory were rewarded in Mexico and Peru with the discovery and conquest of the Aztec and Inca. But they strove in vain to find further riches in the American South and Southwest.

corsair: A pirate on the high seas, or the vessel sailed by pirates.

coureurs de bois: The name given to the French "forest runners"—fur traders and trappers—who ranged far and wide through the Canadian woodlands collecting pelts. Self-reliant and adventure-loving, they adopted the ways of the Indians, and often spent whole years on their own in the depths of the wilderness.

Franciscan: A member of one of the three religious orders founded by Saint Francis of Assisi in the 1200's. Missionaries and teachers, the Franciscans established many outposts in North America, particularly along the California coast, where Father Junípero Serra and his followers founded 21 missions in the 1700's.

hogan: The kind of dwelling used by the Navaho Indians of the Southwest. Hogans were originally made of mud and bark over a conical framework of poles. Today, they are usually made of logs slanted upward from six different sides.

Hopewell culture: One of the best-known prehistoric Indian peoples of the Ohio River Valley region. They possessed a high degree of social organization, and were skilled in the making of tools and elaborate ornaments. The Hopewell operated a vast trade network with other tribes that brought them copper from Lake Superior, shells from the Gulf Coast, obsidian from the Rocky Mountains, and mica from New England. Around A.D. 600, the Hopewell began the custom of housing their dead in large earthen tombs. These burial mounds sometimes contained as many as 1,000 people. In addition, the Ohio Valley Indians built earthworks in the shape of animals, birds, and serpents. Many of these so-called "effigy mounds" can still be seen today.

House of Burgesses: The government of the Virginia colony, and the first representative legislative body in America. It held its first meeting in 1619, and continued to manage the affairs of the colony until 1774, when it was dissolved in order to permit its members to attend the first revolutionary convention in Virginia. The representatives of the house were citizens, or burgesses, elected from the boroughs of Virginia.

intendant: The officer especially appointed by the king of France to head the Sovereign Council (governing body) of New France. Ostensibly, the colonial governor shared the ruling of the colony, but, because the governor was usually occupied with the responsibility of defending New France from the Iroquois, the intendant supervised most of the administration of the Canadian settlement.

Jesuit: A member of the religious order called the Society of Jesus. Founded in 1534 by Saint Ignatius Loyola of Spain, the order soon became world-renowned for its missionary and educational work. The Jesuits were among the most courageous and far-ranging of the Catholic priests who came to America in the 1600's to teach Christianity to the Indians.

kayak: A one-man canoe devised by the Eskimo for fishing and hunting trips. The kayak consists of a light wooden frame tightly covered with a waterproof skin that comes up over the top of the craft and fits snugly around the waist of the occupant.

long house: The type of dwelling used by the Iroquois Indians. Rectangular in shape, the long house consisted of a framework of wooden poles covered over with leaves or bark. A long house could be as much as 100 feet in length, housing up to 20 families, each with its own fireside and sleeping quarters.

Mayflower Compact: An agreement drawn up and signed by the Pilgrim leaders aboard the *Mayflower* before they landed at Plymouth in 1620. The Compact provided for a form of self-government that would ensure discipline in the colony and give the enterprise as a whole some sort of legal basis.

mesa: The Spanish word for "table." Refers to the steep-sided, flat-topped land forms in the American West and Southwest. Created by the erosion of large plateaus, these rocky prominences provided the early pueblo people with natural fortresses.

Mississippian culture: The prehistoric Indian peoples of the Mississippi Valley and the southeastern region of the United States. Primarily farmers, the Mississippians began flourishing about A.D. 1000, just as the Ohio Hopewell culture had begun to decline. The Mississippians possessed a complex religious system centered around the worship of the sun. Their religious centers—square or rectangular wooden temples in which they kept a sacred fire burning—were built on the flat tops of large earthen mounds. The Mississippian and Hopewell peoples are often collectively referred to as the Mound-Builders.

patroon system: A plan initiated by the Dutch West India Company in 1629 to colonize New Netherland—the area now occupied by New York, New Jersey, Connecticut, and Delaware. Under this system, the company granted large tracts of land to wealthy men who would agree to bring over 50 families to work the land. But the only patroonship that ultimately prospered was that of Kiliaen Van Rensselaer on the banks of the Hudson River.

peace pipe: A long-stemmed tobacco pipe used by the American Indians as a symbol of friendship and agreement. At important occasions —a tribal council, or a meeting between the representatives of several tribes— the peace pipe was ceremoniously smoked and passed from hand to hand.

pemmican: A condensed food made by the Plains Indians. It consisted of dried and powdered buffalo meat mixed with hot fat. Berries were often added for flavor. After the mixture had cooled, it was cut into cakes and placed in small bags. Pemmican was rich in nutritional value, and a single bag of it could keep a man alive for many days.

Pilgrim: A member of the group of English settlers who established a colony at Plymouth, Massachusetts in 1620. They were dissatisfied with the kind of Protestantism practiced in England and, because their views had made them unpopular there, had taken up residence in Leyden, Holland for several years (1608–1620). But because they wanted to retain their English way of life and still practice their own form of worship, they decided to found a colony in the New World. The term "Pilgrim," came to be applied to them because they were willing to travel far from home in the cause of their beliefs.

pinnace: A small sailing vessel used chiefly to carry supplies and provisions to larger vessels.

portage: The act of carrying a boat (usually a canoe) or goods overland around unnavigable water, or from one lake or river to another.

potlatch: A ceremonial feast given by a member of one of the Northwest Coast tribes to demonstrate his wealth. At such a feast, he would burn his house, free his slaves, and give away many of his possessions, all the while loudly boasting about how rich he was. A man wealthy enough to hold several potlatches was called a "lord." The possessions he gave away at his feasts became part of the goods that other men, in turn, gave away at their potlatches.

pueblo: The Spanish word for "village." The term is used to refer both to the Pueblo Indians and to their characteristic type of dwelling —a multi-storey, "apartment-house" adobe structure capable of housing all the families of the village. The pueblo had no doors, just holes in the roof, and the ladders used to reach these holes could be pulled up if the pueblo was attacked, turning the dwelling into a fortress.

Puritan: A member of one of the dissenting Protestant sects in England during the 1500's and 1600's. Although the Church of England was Protestant, the Puritans believed that it was still "impure"—still too elaborate and undemocratic. They wanted to do away with church hierarchy and priestly vestments, and get back to a simple form of worship that relied solely on the teachings of the Bible. Some of the Puritans were called "Separatists" because they wanted to break away from the Church of England altogether. The Pilgrims were one such group of Separatists.

royal colony: The term used to describe a colony that had been placed under the direct control of the king. None of the original 13 colonies began as a royal colony. Each was either a proprietary colony (founded and run by a charter-holding individual) or a corporate colony (founded and run by a charter-holding company). By 1775, however, almost all of the 13 colonies had become royal colonies.

scalp bounty: A sum of money paid for an Indian scalp. The early colonial authorities, anxious to reduce the Indian population by fair means or foul, resorted to this method of encouraging the murder of Indians.

scurvy: A disease caused by the lack of vitamin C. Scurvy was extremely common among early mariners who went to sea for long periods of time. Unable to obtain fresh fruit or vegetables countless sailors fell victim to this vitamin-deficiency disease, which can be fatal.

Seven Cities of Cibola: A group of mythical "cities of gold" once believed to exist somewhere in the Americas. It was in search of these cities that the early Spanish conquistadors explored the American South and Southwest.

shaman: The medicine man or priest of certain cultures. The shamans of the American Indian tribes performed ceremonial rites designed to cast out evil spirits, bring good luck, or maintain their people's harmony with the spirit world of nature.

tepee: The type of dwelling used by the Plains tribes. Conical in shape, the tepee was made of buffalo hide stretched over slanting poles and pegged to the ground all the way around the bottom. Tepees were often painted with signs and pictures.

totem: An animal, bird, fish, or plant taken by an Indian tribe, clan, family or individual person as a special symbol. Held as sacred, it was often regarded as the tribe or clan's original ancestor. The tall elaborately carved poles that the Northwest Coast Indians traditionally erected outside their houses were made in honor of their totems.

travois: A means of transportation used by many of the American Indians. It consisted of two long poles with a net lashed between to carry heavy bundles. The travois was pulled by dogs or a horse.

Treaty of Tordesillas: An agreement drawn up by Pope Alexander VI and signed by the monarchs of Spain and Portugal in 1494. According to this agreement, an imaginary north-south line was drawn through the Atlantic Ocean 370 miles west of the Cape Verde Islands. Spain was granted the rights to all newly discovered lands west of this line, while Portugal was given the rights to all newly-discovered lands east of it (including the eastern bulge of Brazil).

walking purchase: A system used by the early Pennsylvania settlers to arrange land purchases from the Indians. According to this system, a settler could purchase as much land as he could walk around in the course of a day and a half.

wigwam: The type of dwelling used by the Algonkian tribes of the Northeast. A wigwam is made of a round or oval-shaped framework of poles covered with a layer of bark or reed mats.

Index

Picture Credits

Listed below are the sources of all the illustrations in this book. To identify the source of a particular illustration, first find the relevant page on the diagram opposite. The number in black in the appropriate position on that page refers to the credit as listed below.

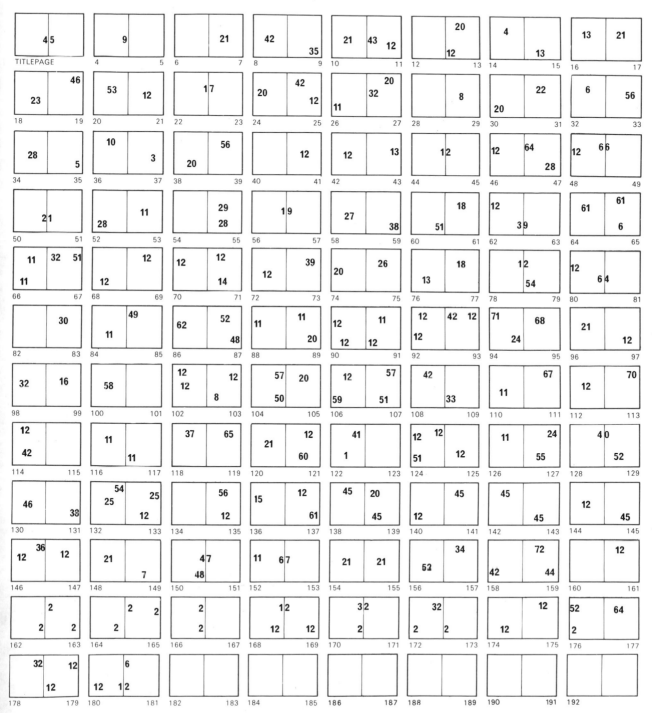